CW00349418

MEMORIES OF
STOCKTON
ON TEES

<u>To our clients, friends and colleagues.</u>

We sponsored this book, about the town where we grew up, in grateful recognition of our parents and what they have done for us, for our children.... and our childrens' children.

<u>Mike, Ken and Tony Devereux</u>

TRUE NORTH BOOKS
DEAN CLOUGH
HALIFAX
WEST YORKSHIRE
HX3 5AX
TEL 01422 344344

THE PUBLISHERS WOULD LIKE TO THANK THE
FOLLOWING COMPANIES FOR SUPPORTING THE
PRODUCTION OF THIS BOOK

MAIN SPONSOR

K.W DEVEREUX & SONS

BRITISH VISQUEEN LIMITED

GRANGEFIELD SCHOOL

HARKERS ENGINEERING LIMITED

LAZENBY'S

PICKERINGS EUROPE LIMITED

CL PROSSER LIMITED

RED HOUSE SCHOOL LIMITED

RELPH FUNERAL SERVICES LIMITED

JOHN RUSSELL & SON (GROCERS) LIMITED

THE IAN RAMSEY SCHOOL

STOCKTON CASTING COMPANY LIMITED

STOCKTON SIXTH FORM COLLEGE

ACKNOWLEDGMENTS

The publishers would like to thank the following individuals and organisations for helping to make
this book possible:
Jack Marriott, who allowed us to reproduce many of his excellent local photographs from the 50s to
the 70s; Mark Rowland-Jones of the Stockton Museums service and his staff; Joyce Chesney and the
staff of the Stockton Reference Library and the staff of the Northern Echo library, in particular Peter
Chapman and Jane Whitfield, who also allowed us to use many of their photographs.

Foreword

Stockton's landscape has changed dramatically in recent years and the pace of change seems likely to continue. This book is a timely reminder therefore of the fascinating heritage we all share. It will bring back memories, not only of places, but of events and people of the past. It will bring much pleasure to many old Stocktonians, like myself, but will also be of great interest to anyone wishing to know more about the town's history.

Although brought up in Norton I attended Holy Trinity School and Stockton Grammar School - since transformed into Ian Ramsey School. In those days they were situated in the centre of town, in Yarm Lane and Norton Road. I therefore spent a great deal of my time from the ages of seven to seventeen exploring the centre of Stockton. I knew all the backstreets around Green Dragon Yard, down past the Empire Theatre, where the Swallow Hotel now stands, and elsewhere. The quayside with its travelling cranes - long since gone - was a constant attraction.

The view from the bottom of Finkle Street next to Walford's offices was entirely industrial. Nothing illustrates more dramatically the changes which have taken place than to stand there today and see the complete transformation of that scene. Both sides of the river have changed beyond recognition, with the new Teesdale bringing developments that were inconceivable only a short time ago. There's plenty of life left in Stockton yet!

Unfortunately not everything that was cleared away from bygone days has left us with a more attractive town. I particularly regret the demolition of the south east side of the High Street with the Vane Arms and the Black Lion in 1970, and the removal of the imposing Victoria Buildings up towards the Parish Church in 1964. They, along with the old-style shops gave a character to the High Street that was attractive and entirely appropriate for the widest high street in the country, dominated as it is by the Parish Church, the Town Hall, the Market Cross and the Shambles. I still have an old overcoat of my father's with the label of Ernest Wimpenny, the old High Street tailor, in it! The more recent improvements in the High Street are welcome but are no substitute for the character which those buildings provided.

But we still have the market. Out of town shopping may provide a lot of things but it cannot match the constant fascination, the variety and hope-for-a-bargain that the market provides. I loved it when I was a kid, rooting around from one end to the other. The Saturday visit to the tripe stall for pigs' trotters, cow heels and different types of tripe that made wonderful meals that I haven't had for years. Lucky *you*, some might say!

These are the sort of indelible memories this book will revive. I am sure it will give great pleasure to all those who read it. Our thanks go to the publishers, and the local organisations that have sponsored it, for making it possible.

Sir Ian Wrigglesworth
Chairman UK Land Estates Ltd
Chairman Northern Business Forum
M.P. Teesside Thornaby & Stockton South, 1974 - 1987

First published in Great Britain by True North Books
Dean Clough
Halifax HX3 5AX
1997

© TRUE NORTH HOLDINGS

ISBN 1 900 463 41 5

Contents

Right: Maxwell's Corner, taken in the late 1950s or early 1960s. The impressive ABC 'Globe' stands at No. 90 High Street, it can be seen here showing the feature 'Who's Minding the Store?' starring Jerry Lewis and the lovely Jill St. John. Sadly the building no longer serves as a cinema.

At your leisure

This photograph dates from 1972, the films being shown at the time were *Chisum* starring John Wayne, and when *Dinosaurs Ruled the Earth* starring someone else. At this time the world of entertainment was more interested in two new productions which had been launched onto the Arts scene. Lloyd Webber's musical *Jesus Christ Superstar* and *Francis Ford Coppola's The Godfather* were to have a much greater impact on the world of entertainment than the makers of *When Dinosaurs Ruled the Earth* could ever have imagined. At the time this scene was recorded this venue was operating under the ownership of the *Essoldo Cinema*, though the word *Hippodrome* was retained on the edge of the canopy in view of its original name when it opened in 1905. For some time the establishment traded as the *Cannon* before closing finally in the last quarter of 1993.

A pleasing view of the Empire Cinema and surrounding buildings which was probably recorded in the early 1950s. An early Landrover can be seen parked on the left of the picture and this allows us to determine that it was taken after 1949. The feature showing at the Empire was Cosh Boy, starring James Cagney and Joan Collins. The supporting feature was 3 Faces West starring John Wayne. Signs advertising the billiards rooms at the Empire can be seen, and further away from the position of the camera is a sign advertising Austin cars from the garage that stood on the site. On the left of the scene Castle's Hat Shop stands beside the cafe next door, and two double decker buses operated by the United Bus Company wait outside. Interestingly, they are carrying advertisements for rival football pools companies - Vernons and Littlewoods. Another advertisement, this time on the right of the picture, informs passers-by that 'opening time is Guinness time'. Finally, we can't leave this picture without a comment on the beautifully-styled street lamp seen in the foreground of the picture. They probably cost a little more than the concrete lamps which replaced them, and would have required painting every so often to keep the rust at bay - but don't they look gorgeous!

Left: The Odeon Cinema was demolished to 'make way for a luxurious new cinema which was in keeping with the modern developments on the High Street' in 1966. The cinema was initially known as the Regal. It opened in April 1935 with a seating capacity of 2000 to much public acclaim. By 1945 Rank took over the business and the name change to *Odeon* took place. The new Odeon was opened in 1968, two years after the demolition of the old building. It traded as a cinema until 1982 when it closed due to falling attendances. Later the building found a new use, as 'The Mall' nightclub.

Many Stockton couples will have fond memories of *courting days* and first dates at the Odeon. Cinemas have a special place in the affections of many people, young and old, and so they should!

Above: Frederic March and Eddie Albert were starring in *The Young Doctors* at the Odeon in the 1960s when this picture was taken. The construction of a new, improved Odeon on this site in 1968 was not enough to reverse the trend of declining audiences and the ultimate closure of the cinema. This pattern of events was not confined to the Stockton area - it had been happening throughout the length and breadth of the country. Many people blamed the rise of T.V, and the launch of colour TV in the 1960s didn't help matters as far as the cinema operators were concerned. Thankfully, and to the surprise of many commentators, cinema-going has seen a recent increase in popularity with the construction of enormous out-of-town multi-screen complexes.

The Secret of Blood Island was the feature showing at the ABC Cinema when this photograph was taken in March 1965. The popular Stockton venue was situated at the northern end of the High Street. It was the third place of entertainment to stand on this site during the 20th century. Initially called The Globe it first saw service as a theatre during the mid 1930s. By 1936 the ABC Cinema Company was showing films here, bowing to the change in demand of the increasingly film-minded audiences of the day. The internal theatre facilities were kept in good order and used for the occasional live opera, ballet and pantomime. Fashions change, and when the film industry itself went into decline the building was turned into a bingo hall and operated by the Mecca organisation.

This well-attended cricket match took place in the suburbs of Stockton in August 1964. These modern Corporation houses were part of the town's growing stock of rented houses, built as part of the drive to replace the rows of badly maintained terraced property which had been the subject of a long running slum clearance programme. Attempts to upgrade the area's housing stock had been made throughout the 1950s and '60s. By 1964 a total of 2500 houses had been pulled down. Records from that year indicate that the Council's plan was to have all the slums cleared by 1968. This involved the removal of a further 2000 properties - a massive undertaking. There had been some considerable success in the provision of new council homes. By 1962 the council was renting out a total of 8700 properties and over three-quarters of these were post-war in origin. Average rents in the mid-1960s were just £2 per week.

> "BY 1962 THE COUNCIL WAS RENTING OUT A TOTAL OF 8700 PROPERTIES.."

On the move

A nostalgic scene from September 1961, featuring some lovely nostalgic vehicles on Bridge Road and the approach to Victoria Bridge. The present bridge dates back to 1887. It was completed at a cost of just over £85,000 and its 60 ft width and 300 ft length made an immediate difference to the flow of traffic into and out of the town. The bridge was floodlit in 1988, and remains an important and impressive part of the historical fabric of the town. The British Road Services flat-backed lorry in this picture would have been a familiar sight to local people in its drab olive green livery. The organisation was hated by independent haulage contractors who were heavily regulated at the time and saw the organisation as a government-sponsored monopoly in the making.

Left: 'Please assist by queuing two deep' was the message at this bus stop. Some of the travelling public of Stockton can be seen doing their best to comply with the request in this picture from 1964. We know from the caption on the back of the print that the scene was captured in December that year, and the headscarves and woolly hats give an indication of how cold it was as the passengers waited for their bus on the Eastbourne Estate route.

Below: 'On the Buses' - Stockton style. Two lovely young ladies pose for the cameraman in this scene from Stockton's public transport archive. It was taken in the mid 1960s. The vehicles seen here were part of a 100 strong fleet of diesel-engined buses owned and operated by Stockton Corporation. Some of the statistics from records kept at the time make interesting reading. The total number of miles travelled by the bus fleet in 1964 was 3,592,820. Working on there being 100 buses in the fleet this means that each vehicle must have travelled around 36,000 mile per year. The records show that there were 41,000,000 passenger-journeys during the year. It is interesting to look back on the events which were shaping Britain at the time this picture was taken; the 'Great Train Robbers' received heavy sentences in 1964 and Britain's first lady Member of Parliament, Lady Astor, died. Winston Churchill made his last appearance in Parliament and the Commons voted to end capital punishment. This was also the year that Nelson Mandella started his long term of imprisonment and the American Film star Alan Ladd died.

Above: A nostalgic view from the mid-1960s which features a group of ladies on their way home from a shopping trip in the town centre. The bus in question is the No. 8 Roseworth service operated by the Corporation Transport Department. It is seen at the bus stop outside Timothy Whites, the popular high street chemist chain which later became absorbed in the *Boots* organisation.

Below: A milestone in the history of Stockton's local transport arrangements was passed in 1964 when a fleet of seven new double deckers like the one seen here were purchased by the Corporation. The new vehicles were part of the 100-strong fleet operated by the Corporation and had many modern features which made them an instant hit with the travelling public. One innovation took the form of the entrance to the bus which had a gradual slope rather than steps to allow easier access. A sophisticated heating system ensured that all the passengers were kept warm in winter and, uniquely, it doubled as an effective cooling system during the hot weather. It was said that mums with small children appreciated the spiral staircase which had no awkward corners to get in the way of their shopping bags and prams. The vehicles cost £7000 each - around 10% more than the 'buses they replaced, and an order for another 13 units the following year. All in all, the buses received a huge 'thumbs up' from the people of Stockton.

In 1964 the vandalism we see on our public transport system - and elsewhere - was less common than we experience today. Indeed, even the *term* 'vandalism' was uncommon then.

An early Austin Luton-bodied furniture van built by Marsdens of Warrington and operated by K.W Devereux and Sons. This type of vehicle body is referred to as a 'Luton' when the box-shaped area at the back extends over the top of the drivers' cab. Many drivers would, on occasion, use this void as a place to sleep on long journeys when an overnight stay was involved. Because of this a saying evolved, and drivers would often tell their friends that they were staying 'in the Luton Hotel' when referring to their makeshift

"DRIVERS WOULD OFTEN TELL THEIR FRIENDS THEY WERE STAYING IN THE LUTON HOTEL..."

sleeping arrangements. Interestingly, the Billingham address shown on the side of the furniture van is given as 'Marsh House Avenue.' There is a story behind this. When *Devereux* acquired the site in Billingham they were told that it would be called Marsh House Avenue ..and painted their vehicles accordingly. At the last minute the planners changed their minds about the layout of the industrial estate, and the roads which were initially supposed to be at the front of each unit ended up at the rear. Thus, the correct address for the new premises became Leeholme Road..... and the vehicles were repainted accordingly.

The distinctive corner turret of the Yorkshire Bank building, located at 46, High Street. Of course the Yorkshire Bank remains, at the time of writing at least, in business on this busy corner of the High Street in this very stylish property. The first floor of the bank was occupied by the administrative and sales staff of the Pearl Assurance Company. An Austin A30 van standing just outside the bank leads us to believe that the picture was taken in the late 1950s. The photograph gives a rare view of Charles Clinkard Ltd the shoe retailer which stood along Finkle Street for many years. At the bottom of Finkle Street a tall crane can be seen beside the River Tees, evidence that Stockton was still active as a port when the picture was taken. This very unusual picture gives a dramatic rooftop view of the area leading up to the industrialised quayside, long before anyone dreamed of cleaning up the site and making it a centre of learning, relaxation and recreation.

A family day out would often begin on the platform of a railway station, where anxious mums would keep tight hold of the hands of their little ones. Even better would be the excitement felt when the family was about to depart on a weeks' holiday at a coastal resort. This appears to be the case for some of the passengers waiting here, judging by the collection of suitcases lined up beside the people in the centre of the photograph.

The picture was taken in 1962 at Thornaby railway station. The group in the centre of the scene is made up of members of the Bainbridge family. The lady with the white handbag and the coat over her arm is Mrs Dorothy Bainbridge, Lena Bainbridge is slightly to the left, holding the hand of her grandson Robert Bainbridge.

We are grateful to Mrs Dorothy Bainbridge for allowing us to reproduce this photograph in the book.

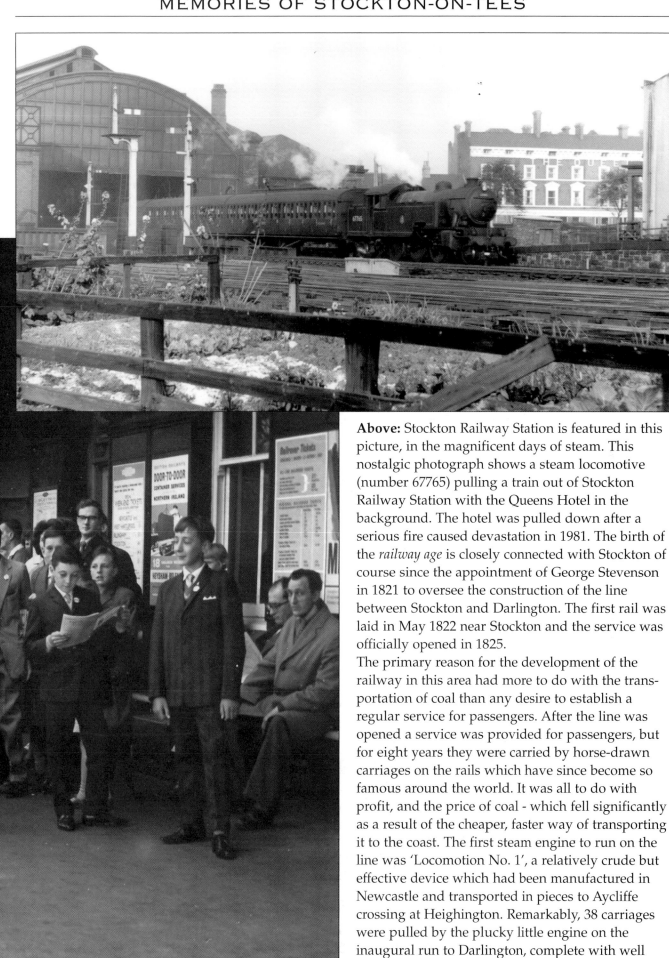

Above: Stockton Railway Station is featured in this picture, in the magnificent days of steam. This nostalgic photograph shows a steam locomotive (number 67765) pulling a train out of Stockton Railway Station with the Queens Hotel in the background. The hotel was pulled down after a serious fire caused devastation in 1981. The birth of the *railway age* is closely connected with Stockton of course since the appointment of George Stevenson in 1821 to oversee the construction of the line between Stockton and Darlington. The first rail was laid in May 1822 near Stockton and the service was officially opened in 1825.

The primary reason for the development of the railway in this area had more to do with the transportation of coal than any desire to establish a regular service for passengers. After the line was opened a service was provided for passengers, but for eight years they were carried by horse-drawn carriages on the rails which have since become so famous around the world. It was all to do with profit, and the price of coal - which fell significantly as a result of the cheaper, faster way of transporting it to the coast. The first steam engine to run on the line was 'Locomotion No. 1', a relatively crude but effective device which had been manufactured in Newcastle and transported in pieces to Aycliffe crossing at Heighington. Remarkably, 38 carriages were pulled by the plucky little engine on the inaugural run to Darlington, complete with well over 300 passengers on board. Darlington was reached in just over an hour, and the subsequent journey on to Stockton - a distance of 12 miles - took a further three hours and seven minutes.

A sunny 1950s view of the High Street which succeeds perfectly in capturing the atmosphere of the time. The lovely old vehicles in the scene add to our nostalgic thoughts as we study the once familiar buildings along Stockton's favourite street. They are reminiscent of 1950s black and white films and one can almost hear the sound of whining gearboxes and axles as the plucky little motors make their way around the town. The Black Lion can be seen on the right of the picture, and other businesses on that side of the High Street include the tobacconists next door, followed by the florists, run for many years by and The Vane Arms, Chippendale House, Pickersgill's Ironmongers and H & W. Martin the 'sporting tailors.'

A moving force around the World

A visit to K.W Devereux and Sons is a revealing experience. Devereux's bright red trucks have been spotted by local people on their travels in all parts of Britain for as long as most people can remember. It is not uncommon for them to be seen in Europe now, and the *Devereux* service is legendary among customers as far away as Australia and North America. The company has grown from a one-man operation more than fifty years ago to one which has international connections and real influence in the world of road haulage and removals. Yet the people in charge of Devereux in the 1990s have their feet firmly on the ground and have not lost sight of the fact that it is the hard work, expertise and loyalty of their staff which continues to attract and retain the firm's biggest asset - satisfied customers. Mr. Mike Devereux, one of the three sons of the founder, stresses the importance of the *family business* ethos which drives the whole operation. He feels a genuine responsibility for the security of every family connected with the firm and makes no secret of it. "Without our drivers and support staff in every part of the business we simply *wouldn't have* a business" he says. The staff of 140 includes many brothers, fathers and sons who work with their relatives under the Devereux banner. It is a family firm in every sense of the word, and that special relationship based on trust and commitment enables the company to score over its rivals on many different fronts. The presence of long-serving employees is a good indication of the health of a company. At Devereux this is encouraged to the extent to which a 'Rolex Club' has been formed by the staff who have been awarded the prized time-piece after serving 25 years. Members of the *club* get a friendly roasting from their colleagues if they forget to wear their watch at one of the company get-togethers!

K.W. Devereux & Sons is recognised as being in the *premier league* of removal and haulage companies. But this strong competitive position has only been made possible by the vision and determination of the firm's founding father, Ken Devereux, and the story of how he started and grew the business from a very early age makes fascinating reading.

Ken Devereux started working for himself in 1934 when he was just 14 years old. The law of the land dictated that you had to be 21 in order to run a business, so Ken persuaded his father, Henry, who worked at ICI at the time, to record his name on the official forms. At the age of 78 Ken Devereux is still involved in the business, limited these days to a few hours every week, but he did work full-time until he was 75! His participation in the business is a labour of love for Ken; "sitting in front of the T.V all day would drive me up the wall!" he said.

The firm had very humble origins; what Ken didn't know about business he made up for with an eye for an opportunity and the boundless energy of a single-minded teenager. The early years were tough and unglamorous; the first business activity undertaken by the young Ken Devereux

to the handcart hire concept, ladders being the kind of equipment that people required only occasionally, were durable and uncomplicated, and could be hired out to some of the contacts already made in his existing business. The investment was made and soon began to make a worthwhile contribution to the developing firm.

The business was now operating out of a timber yard in Norton and as the years went by Ken's father was able to leave his job at ICI and work full-time with his son. A variety of building-related products was on offer here, including sand, cement, timber etc., and the business was known as *The Handyman's Store*. The firewood, handcart and ladder-hire side of the business had enabled the business to grow and built a reputation for reliability and keen prices. It also provided the capital for Ken to make the most significant move in the early development of the firm.... the purchase of his first commercial motor vehicle.

Ken remembers buying the vehicle, second-hand, from Wheatleys of Stockton in 1937. The van had previously been used by Berry's the butcher of Wolviston. It was too small for much of the work Ken had lined up for it, so he set about it, using his carpentry skills, and cut the rear body off the van. A hole was cut into the front of the vehicle so that longer pieces of timber could be accommodated. Ken picked up useful motor body-building skills in the conversion of his first truck which proved an advantage in future years. Ken remembers proudly that this vehicle was the first pick-up truck to be used in the North East. Motorised distribution took off and

involved delivering a variety of goods by handcart. Firewood was one of the most regular products to be wheeled through the streets of Norton, but soon whole house removals, and even pianos, would find their way on to the top of this most basic transport. Ken and the occasional helper became a regular sight grunting and straining with their heavy loads on the roads around the area. The business developed through the 1930s and Ken remembers how people would enquire if they could hire a handcart to do their own house removals, an obvious attempt to keep the cost down, and very similar to the 'self-drive' van hire services of modern times. Ken saw this as a way of building up his business without doing all the work himself, and developed this service to the point where he had 10 handcarts regularly hired out by the public and by small traders. At the time, a handcart was sufficient for the removal needs of most local folk. The handcart hiring side of the business flourished and Ken sought ways of investing the profits into a new line which would help the firm grow even more. He hit upon the idea of hiring out ladders. There were obvious similarities

*Above: Young Michael with Peter the dog taking an early interest in dad's trucks in the late 1940s. **Right:** A petrol voucher issued in the 1950s when rationing was still in force around the country. **Facing page, top centre:** The Devereux family in the early 1960s L-R Barbara, Ken, KW, Tony, Catherine, Mike. **Facing page, bottom left:** A truly nostalgic picture. A 1934 Austin 10 van in original Devereux livery which is still in the company's possession today.*

soon Ken was able to consider the purchase of an additional vehicle. It came in the form of a sturdy 30 cwt Chevrolet which was fully utilised in the growing haulage business, delivering model boats from Harkers of Danby Road to Newcastle. A contract was secured with Seymours,

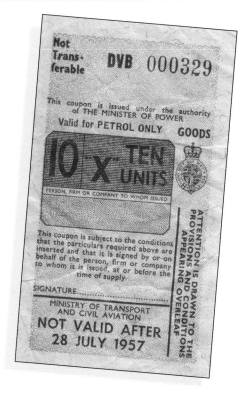

Not Transferable   DVB 000329

This coupon is issued under the authority of THE MINISTER OF POWER

Valid for PETROL ONLY   GOODS

10 "X" TEN UNITS

PERSON, FIRM OR COMPANY TO WHOM ISSUED

This coupon is subject to the conditions that the particulars required above are inserted and that it is signed by or on behalf of the person, firm or company to whom it is issued, at or before the time of supply.

SIGNATURE

MINISTRY OF TRANSPORT AND CIVIL AVIATION

NOT VALID AFTER 28 JULY 1957

ATTENTION IS DRAWN TO THE PROVISIONS AND CONDITIONS APPEARING OVERLEAF

the steel distributors who had their works at the Phoenix Sidings in Stockton, and the business began to gather momentum. Furniture removals remained an important part of the business and the transition from transportation by handcart to the more efficient motor van was seamless. Ken Devereux remembers how the removal trade has changed over the years: "old ladies would often try and do us a favour by emptying their cupboards and chests of drawers. This was usually no help at all, because they put all the contents into the wardrobe, which they would then lock....and we would find it almost impossible to lift because of the tremendous weight!" Often, on arriving at a house we would be asked to take down the T.V aerial and put it up again at the 'new' house. The same would apply to coal in the days where coal fires were the norm. "Sometimes the customer would ask us to load half a ton of coal in the back of the van, along with their furniture" said Mr. Devereux with a bemused look in his eye.

The narrow, terraced houses had steep staircases and it was often difficult to remove furniture from the upper floor. The answer was simple, to remove the sash window and take the bed, wardrobe and other furniture though it. Ken even fitted platforms on top of his early removal vans which would allow the men to carefully manoeuvre the items from the house and into the van. The arrival of casement windows in the 1960s, along with furniture which could be taken apart to facilitate easier removal, made these high level removal procedures rather less frequent. Everything was in place for steady growth and continued development, but in 1939 the outbreak of war threw Ken Devereux's plans into disarray.

Ken Devereux was just 20 years old when the prospect of war loomed in 1939. Initially the call-up offered a choice of serving in the Territorials, doing nightly duties for 6 months or serving full-time in the Regular Army for two years. Following advice from his father Ken decided that he should enlist full time and get his military service out of the way. It was July 1939. Things didn't work out quite the way he planned, for in September war was declared, and it was not until *six years* later that he was demobbed.

The war years initially saw Ken Devereux shipped off to France, then to North Africa. He was badly wounded in the battle of El Alamein from where he was taken, on the Dutch Hospital Ship *Oranges* to Durban, South Africa and then transferred to the hospital in Pietermaritzburg. There he spent eight long months recovering from his injuries, always hopeful that the next journey would be back to the North East of England. This was not to be, and Ken was transferred to a posting in Cairo on his discharge from hospital, working for the elite, top secret A-Force - the team of ingenious masters of deception which would later form the basis of MI5. Ken has

fond memories of the leader of the A-Force, Major Jasper Maskelyne the famous illusionist who ran his own London theatre before the outbreak of war. All manner of tricks and deceptions were directed at the enemy, ranging from creating artificial tank divisions in the desert, to the construction of huge dummy submarines in ports to give the enemy the wrong impression about the Allies intentions. The work was varied, and this helped keep Ken's mind active as the war progressed. During the war Ken returned to the north east and married Catherine his wife of over 50 years. His thoughts, however, were never very far away from his wife and business back in England, and Ken spent many hours dreaming about how he would develop the transport firm he had started on his return to 'civvy street.'

The end of the war was welcome news for everyone, and when Ken returned home he found that his father Henry had succeeded in keeping the business running well. More than this, before long Henry Devereux seemed to have achieved the impossible in the period just after the war - he had managed to locate and agree to purchase a new 5 ton Austin truck for Ken.   Initially, business was very slow. It was for everyone in industry as the economy gradually got back into swing. Ken knew that if his business was to succeed he had to find a steady flow of income that

he could rely on - and find it quickly. Ken discovered that the MPRD (the Ministry responsible for the allocation of scarce resources at the time) was selling off wooden crates at their depot at Early Nook Railway Station. These crates had contained aircraft parts during the war and were now no longer needed. He knew also that new timber was in short supply, only available on licence - and in great demand; this gave him an idea. He bought the crates at favourable prices and took them to pieces to sell to eager buyers around the district. At the same time he grasped every chance for haulage work, often taking on jobs at very low margins, just to get some momentum in his business again. The difficulties in the haulage business were compounded by the fact that fuel was still rationed after the end of the war. Rationing continued up until the mid 1950s.

Government restrictions and strict licensing laws added to the problems faced by road hauliers and

Opposite page bottom left: Ken Devereux at the wheel of a WWII Willys Jeep.
Opposite page above: A romantic wartime picture showing Cath and Ken Devereux soon after they were married.
Above: Jasper Maskelyne, the wartime hero and friend of Ken Devereux pictured in London.

Above: Devereux's distinctive Britannia-liveried vehicles seen here at the official opening of Devereux Driver Training Services by Tony Blair.

many went out of business. Up until this time Ken Devereux had been working with his father out of the open timber yard at Norton. Timber reclamation and sales had been an important part of the business so far, but Ken Devereux wanted to concentrate on the haulage side of the firm. To this end, in the late 1940s, he took the decision to leave the yard and go into haulage full-time. His father Henry remained there and ran the business for a further 5 years or so until it was sold as a going concern.

The new yard was located at Crisp Street, Norton, at the back of the Brown Jug. The operational side was run from here while Cath, Ken's wife, ran the office and all the administration from their home in Norton Road. Cath continued to do this for many years until the business relocated to Leeholme Road in Billingham. Ken set about the task of securing new contracts for his growing firm. Airex Fans Ltd., a Sheffield company based at Phoenix Sidings, was an early customer and work for them took the company all over the country. It was a turning point for K.W Devereux and Sons and represented their first really big contract. Ken remembers how they would deliver the enormous ventilation fans to the London Underground system when new lines were being constructed. Another major contract was secured from Stilite Products Ltd., (manufacturers of slag wool, used as insulation material) and this involved the distribution of the light, but very bulky product to most parts of the United Kingdom.

The business continued to develop during the 1950s, and valuable contracts were secured with several local firms including furnishers Jays, Woodhouses and Barker and Stonehouse. Removals, using lorries with 'Luton' bodies remained a valuable part of the business. Ken Devereux put the carpentry skills he had acquired to good use in this respect. During quiet periods he would build the bodies for his vehicles using timber frames and aluminium sheeting. This naturally led to another strand of the business, buying ex-W D trucks from the government depot in Ruddington Park near Nottingham, doing any repairs necessary and selling them on. The strong ex-army Bedford trucks were ideally suited to use as tippers. Bedfords were popular with small business proprietors - "every small businessman owned a Bedford at some time during their life" said Ken, "especially in the removal trade - even Pickfords used them."

The tippers came in handy when a contract was won to work on the site of the Lacenby Steel Works in the early 1960s. This involved transporting building materials and removing thousands of tons of excavated material from the site. Taking slag from the slag heaps and delivering it to the area which would become the foundations was another important part of the work.

The virtual nationalisation of the road haulage industry by the creation of British Road Services after the war made life challenging for those committed to independent road haulage. Various licenses were required for the private firms to operate, all designed to create and protect the BRS monopoly. Special exemptions could be applied for specific customers to the local Traffic Commissioner at the Magistrates Courts. Licenses were expensive but essential if the firm was to stay in business. Even now, Ken Devereux has strong feelings about the

regulation of road haulage industry. "It should be left to people who know what they're talking about; you can't expect Transport Ministers to be any good at their job if they have no experience. Its too complicated and too important to be left to amateurs. The whole industry should be regulated on a non-political basis" The epitome of bad judgement in this respect was the appointment of Barbara Castle as a Minister of Transport in the 1960s. "She didn't even have a driving licence!" said Ken with incredulity.
The growing reputation of K.W Devereux and Sons led to increasing business in the 1960s and 1970s and the end of close regulation from the licensing author-

ities enabled further investment to be made. The first big order for lorries came during this period and Ken agreed to buy three Ford D1000s with extended, rigid bodies. Later he supplemented his growing fleet with articulated Ford lorries with powerful tractor units which could easily cope with the ever increasing distances being travelled. A contract was secured with Henderson Doors of Bowburn at around this time and the business flourished.

Since his retirement from the day-to-day running of the company, Ken Devereux has piece of mind from the knowledge that the firm is now under the stewardship of his three sons, Mike, Ken and Tony. Mike has been involved in the business since the late 1950s. He remembers his father saying 'I started work at 14 Mike... and if it was good enough for me

Above: Prior to furniture being moved abroad in containers, Devereux would pack and crate everything. The two large crates seen here were part of a large consignment bound for Philadelphia USA.
Left: Devereux's proud boast "we move anything anywhere" was tested to the extreme when part of the family consignment included several hives of bees. Seen here, holding a hive-full were the "fearless" (R-L) Gordon Metcalf and Denny Brown, while Denny's brother Ralph ensures that the bees have a quiet ride.

then you can too. ' Not that Mike needed much encouragement. After doing odd -jobs after school and at weekends, and gaining a thorough grounding in every aspect of the business, he couldn't wait to get his driving licence. Initially he gained his licence for cars and then his HGV licence. In later years Ken joined the business, followed by his brother Tony. Ken now heads the road haulage side of the firm with his brother Tony.

1993 saw a milestone in the development of the company which attracted recognition for the high degree of quality achieved in all aspects of its operations.

Sir Ian Wrigglesworth, chairman of the northern CBI, presented K.W Devereux & Sons with the British Standards certification of quality BS5750. Norton-born Sir Ian has experienced the service for which the firm has become well known many times as a *Devereux* customer himself. It was particularly pleasing therefore when he said that he was 'delighted but not at all surprised' at the company's achievement. 'On the basis of my experience Devereux being awarded BS5750 is simply a confirmation of their excellent track record. Quite simply, the service they provide is of the highest quality."

In true Devereux style the company did not follow

the usual route of gaining the BS5750 award in stages. Normally companies do the work and apply for BS5750 for one aspect of their operation - say road haulage, and add further departments and services gradually. K.W Devereux & Sons took the bold step of seeking accreditation for the whole of their business activities at the same time - road haulage, warehousing, distribution, storage, worldwide freight and shipping. The BSI assessor, responsible for accrediting companies, paid tribute to the tremendous amount of work involved. He described the firm as 'an outstanding company' and said that he was extremely impressed by the professionalism at Devereux.

There are many challenges facing the removal and haulage industries and K W Devereux & Sons has played a leading part in fighting the cause through several leading trade associations. As founder members of Britannia Movers International in 1981 this Company led the drive to get a fair deal and a professional service for members -and their clients- in the world of international shipping. The organisation had its first headquarters in Stourbridge in the West Midlands, and is run along limited company lines, with each member taking a shareholding. Initially the organisation was successful in securing more favourable terms with Shippers to the most popular overseas destinations, but since then its power and influence has grown. In 1985 Mike Devereux's contribution to the association was recognised when he was elected Chairman, a position he maintained for 7 years. This was not the end of Mike Devereux's contribution to the development of the industry, for he went on immediately to become the President of another leading body, the British Association of Removers. This trade association is widely recognised as the guardian of the highest standards of operating practice in the removal world. All applicants are vetted and monitored to ensure that they are worthy of membership, and in a position to uphold the trading practices and reputation built up by existing members. Areas scrutinised include training, insurance arrangements, vehicle licensing and maintenance, and compliance with various elements of legislation. Obtaining membership of B.A.R is difficult, unlike membership of some trade organisations which offer a thinly-veiled cloak of respectability in return for an annual fee. Clients using a B.A.R member enjoy an arbitration service in the event of a dispute, in addition to the peace of mind which results from knowing the remover works to the highest possible standards. K.W Devereux and Sons is a member of many other trade associations, the Road Haulage Association, The Freight Transport Association and the Transport Association. F.I.D.I. (The International Movers Association), The Professional Movers Association of South Africa, The Canadian Association of Movers and The National Moving and Storage Association of America.

The management and staff at Devereux are proud of their past and the achievements made since the company was started by Ken Devereux all those years ago. But that does not mean that the firm is backward-looking. In fact, quite the opposite is true. One of the proudest moments in the recent history of the firm was the opening of the new Devereux Driver Training Services by the Rt. Hon Tony Blair M.P., not long before he went on to take up the office of Prime Minister. The idea of creating a driving school for

heavy goods vehicle drivers sprang out of the company's own needs to assess the capabilities of prospective drivers, and to continually develop skills of the existing driving team in all aspects of their work including defensive driving. An experienced trainer was appointed and a training vehicle was assigned for the job. As the training side of the business grew a second trainer was appointed to specialise in the 'classroom' and theoretical side of the process which included the ADR qualification relating to the safe transportation of chemical substances. Legislation demands that all drivers of chemical loads must have the ADR certificate. Other vehicles have been added to the training fleet to teach additional HGV classifications. Since the start of the new service the Training Centre has enjoyed considerable success and has attracted customers from other haulage companies in the North East.

The opening day was a great success and everyone at the company was proud to see that Civic Dignitaries from four Boroughs were in attendance along with local MP Frank Cook (a former Devereux employee) and the leader of the Labour Party and Parliamentary Member for Sedgefield Tony Blair MP. The future P.M drove a tractor unit around the yard and took part in a fire- fighting demonstration in which he extinguished a controlled fire. The day was a huge success and will be remembered by everyone who attended for many years to come, but especially by Mr. Ken Devereux, the man who set the ball rolling as an energetic 14 year old, back in 1934.

Above: Another company milestone was the opening of its new Driver Training Centre earlier this year by Tony Blair MP, shortly before he became Prime Minister. Left to right: Tony Blair MP, Christine Devereux, Cath Devereux, Frank Cook MP, Tony Devereux and Ken Devereux. Facing page, top right: In 1993, the company was awarded BS5750. Left to right: Tony Devereux, Mike Devereux, Mike Babinski, Sir Ian Wrigglesworth and Ken Devereux. Facing page, bottom: One of the new vehicles in the fleet, still with its distinctive red and white livery.

Around the town centre

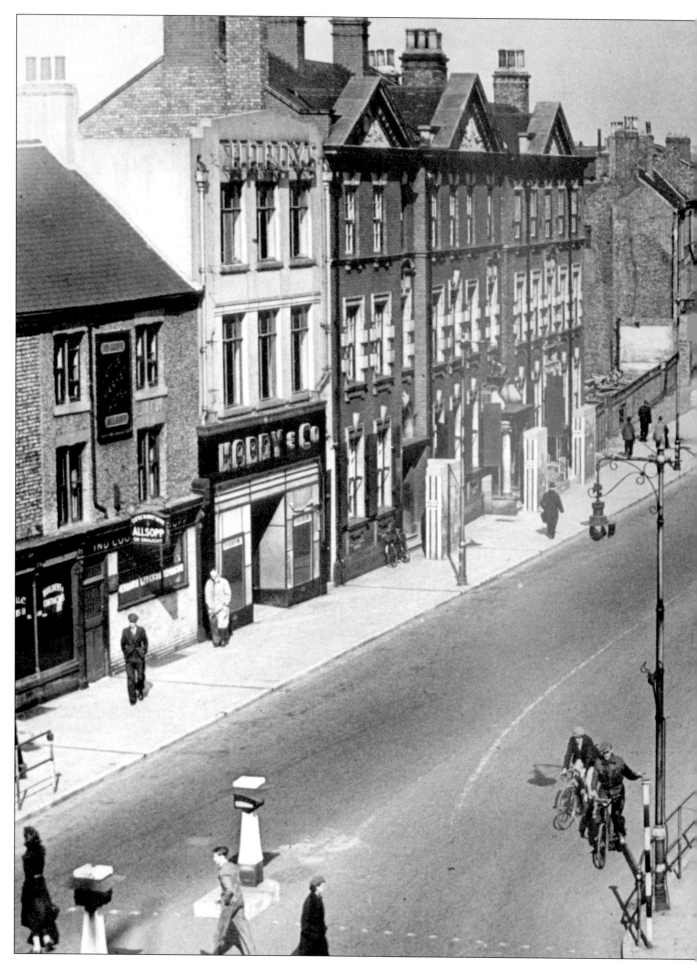

"STOCKTON WAS THE TARGET OF THE NAZI BOMBERS ON SEVERAL OCCASIONS DURING THE WAR"

A slightly elevated 1940s view of the Cattle Market Hotel and Hardy and Co. next door. Of course this area of Church Road has seen many changes since the picture was taken, with the building of the Swimming Baths and Public Library and Council Buildings. It is thought that the picture was taken during the war years. Stockton was the target of the Nazi bombers on several occasions during the war. In 1941 an air raid on the town resulted in the death of about eight local people when houses were destroyed near St, Peter's Church on Yarm Road. Bombs fell on Stockton later in the war; in all a total of 21 civilians lost their lives and around 200 houses were reduced to rubble.

Above: It was a sad day for Stockton when the decision was taken to demolish the Vane Arms Hotel and the adjoining buildings. This picture gives a good view of the establishment, standing as it did beside Laesers the chocolate shop and Masterman's next door. On the right of the picture it is just possible to see the corner of William's Florists shop. *Ogden's of Otley* were the main contractors for the demolition work in 1970 and their heavy tipper trucks became a familiar sight to local people as they carted off hundreds of tons of rubble which once made up many of the fine old buildings pictured in this book. The changes which took place enabled the planners top create the modern new shopping centre and open spaces we know now, with wide walkways, seating and trees which symbolised the architectural shopping revolution of the '60s and '70s. Stockton High Street has changed considerably, but thankfully it has not lost the essential character which has set it apart from that of neighbouring towns for over a century.

Below: The Royal Oak situated at 19 High Street dominates this photograph from the 1960s. The wet cobbles add to the character of the scene, and the side of Victoria Buildings can be seen on the right of the picture, complete with the hairdressing salon which traded under the name of *Lilyan and Betty* for many years. The appearance of the Royal Oak, a Bass House, has been transformed into a modern square-frontage in more recent times. A well-known high street bank operated from the building on the left of the pub, with the offices of the Prudential Assurance company above it, along with the headquarters of Robert B. Bainbridge the builder. The bank no longer trades as such but thankfully the delightful bow window can still be seen. On the right of the Royal Oak there was an Avery Weighing Scale sales office. These were a familiar sight on the streets of many northern towns at one time, serving hundreds of small and large shops in the days before most goods came pre-weighed and pre-packed. The distinctive building on the corner of this block, near Victoria Buildings, was the Trustee Savings Bank, formerly the 'Savings Bank of Newcastle upon Tyne.'

Above: An early 1950s view of the Royal Hotel and the adjacent shop premises leading to the corner of the Empire Cinema on the right of the picture. The Empire's billiard hall entrance is just in view, as is the Castle Cafe, Castle hat shop and C.W Laws. The Royal Hotel was one of the town's oldest hotels - it had been in existence since 1740 - almost fifty years *before* the French Revolution! This long history was not enough to save it though, as the 1960s put new demands on the High Street and on hotel-keeping. By 1962 the property had been earmarked for demolition.

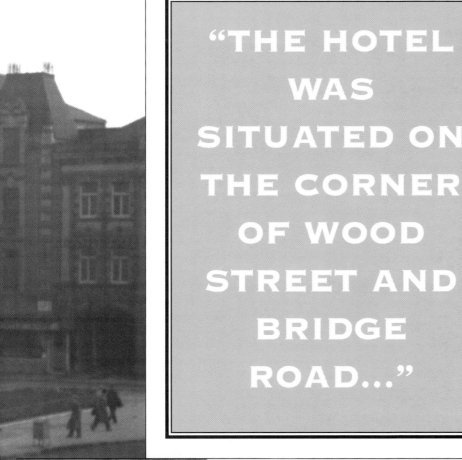

"THE HOTEL WAS SITUATED ON THE CORNER OF WOOD STREET AND BRIDGE ROAD..."

Below: The Hotel Metropole was situated on the corner of Wood Street and Bridge Road. The hotel enjoyed an excellent reputation and was widely recognised as one of the leading hotels in the district. This picture is believed to date from around the mid 1960s, one clue being the registration mark of the mini-van in the picture, the 'B' suffix making it at least 1964. The building was pulled down in order to make way for Daryl House, now the location of Stockton's Job Centre.

Above: Thirsty Stockton drinkers could be sure of a friendly welcome at the Grey Horse. The picture shows the popular inn on the corner Yarm Lane and the High Street. This site was within staggering distance of around a dozen other well-supported watering holes when this picture was taken in the 1960s. The Regal cinema was nearby and this made it handy for people wanting a quick drink before watching their favourite film. The Ford Prefect van on the left of the picture was the trusty workhorse for thousands of small business people throughout the country. It was one of the first small commercial vehicles to offer the comfort and styling of the equivalent saloon car. The main competitor to this vehicle was the Morris Minor van which dominated the market and remains highly prized among classic car enthusiasts. More Minor's have survived than the Ford pictured here, and the Anglia van which eventually replaced it.

Below: The focal point of this 1950s photograph is the lovely curvaceous charabanc making its way towards the Shambles, past rows of busy market stalls. The aluminium bodied vehicle with its full length fabric roof would have been quite a novelty at the time. In the distance, on the right, another interesting vehicle can just be seen. It is an ex-army truck, one of many surplus vehicles sold off by the War Department to local traders in the years after the end of the war. On the left of the picture the sign denoting the location of the Stockton Cinema is just visible. The photograph affords a good view of the Shambles and the Town Hall in the distance as it appeared on a busy market day. Looking back on the 1950s we remember that this was a decade where, despite the fairly recent end of the Second World War, peace seemed to elude the world and the threat of a return to war was never far from our minds. This was the decade of *Suez* and the start of the cold war between East and West; many of the people walking along Stockton High Street in this picture would have been concerned about the threat posed by the events taking place on the world stage as well as by developments much closer to home.

A delightful view looking across towards Maxwell's Corner, taken in the late 1950s or early 1960s. The Castle and Anchor, a Vaux public house, can be seen in the foreground, on the right, at the end of Church Road. The impressive ABC 'Globe' stands at No. 90 High Street, it can be seen here showing the feature 'Who's Minding the Store?' starring Jerry Lewis and the lovely Jill St. John. Sadly the building no longer serves as a cinema and is offered for the sale at the time of writing. For a time after 1978 the building served as a bingo hall, but even this was not commercially successful enough to preserve its role as a popular place of entertainment. Next to the ABC, further away from the camera in this picture, the modern building housing W. Duncan's Supermarket can be seen just past Middle Street. In the block housing Maxwell's School Outfitters, which gave the corner its name, Sam's Friendly Furnishers and the G-Plan centre can be seen.

Above: A mid-1960s view along Church Road, taken from the roof of the Parish Church. Work had already started on making this area the modern 'municipal' heart of Stockton. The Municipal Buildings were opened in 1961 and later extended in the late 1980s. The Library building on the right of Church Road was opened in 1969. Council Offices (in the form of Gloucester House) would be added along with the new Public Swimming Baths in the late 1960s which would transform the appearance of this area completely. The YMCA building was opened by Her Majesty the Queen in March 1968. Many of the buildings on the left of Church Road, in the distance, remain to this day, along with the garage on the opposite side of the road which now serves as a quick-fit tyre, exhaust and battery centre. On the left of the picture the grey outline of a gas holder can be made out in the middle distance.

Below: Shoppers queue for their bus on the way home from a hard day's bargain hunting. The Town Hall can be seen in the distance on this picture from the mid-1960s. On the left of the picture it may just be possible to read the sign on the large white building which identifies it as Blacketts department store. This was a favourite among Stockton shoppers in its hey-day, but sadly the store was pulled down in 1972 as part of the wholesale changes which affected the town centre in the late 1960s and 1970s. Other department stores responded to the opening of the *Castle Centre* and the threat that this posed to them by increasing the sales floor space on their premises. The Castle Centre therefore had a far greater effect on Stockton's shopping environment than many people predicted at first, as the competitive spirit was aroused in every business involved in the town's retail trade - generally to the benefit of the shopping public.

This picture from the 1960s is bound to bring back fond memories of shopping trips to this block of Stockton shops. Book's was popular among ladies wishing to make an impression at a special occasion - they were noted for the quality of the stock they carried. George's Cash Discount Store next door sold curtains and home furnishings. Peter's Army and Navy Stores sold everything you could ever need to combat bad weather - from donkey jackets and farmers coats to 'shortie coats', as well as the usual sleeping bags, primus stoves, ground sheets and other camping needs. Rain wear was also the main stock-in-trade for Stewart's Mac Shop next door. There rather depressing slogan 'we shall have rain' would have been familiar to Stockton people. A sign in the window at Stewarts informs us that this is 'Coat Week.'

Below: The early 1960s and a familiar view along Stockton's High Street. This was a prime stretch of retail property at the time. In common with most towns of any size, the area immediately surrounding the *Marks and Spencer* store was always popular with other retailers, keen to exploit the attraction of shoppers to this location by Britain's most successful retailer. Timothy Whites chemist stood next to W.H Smiths the booksellers on the High Street. Timothy Whites was taken over by Boots the massive Nottingham-based retail chemists (their Stockton branch can be seen further up the High Street) and W.H Smiths moved into the Castle shopping centre in the 1970s. Stead and Simpsons the popular shoe retailers were further along the High Street with the Midland Bank and Littlewoods department store beyond that. The Ford Consul cars in the picture would have been the object of dreams for many youngsters and their dads. The big wallowing saloons became an icon of the day, before rises in the cost of petrol made us all rather more conscious of our fuel consumption.

Right: The Yorkshire Penny Bank building as it appeared in the early 1960s. Though not as large as many high street banks it has always had a stylish

facade giving it a character which has set it apart from many of the more clinical properties which have served the world of banking. In this picture the offices of the Pearl Assurance Company can be seen above the bank, and the smaller offices of Lax and Wright insurance agents are visible on the right of the picture. Below this was a vetinary surgeons' practice.

Below: Dating from the early 1950s this traffic scene in Stockton shows three well-known retail outlets, Greenwoods (the mens' wear specialists), Maynards and Clydesdale the cycle and radio shop. It seems strange to us now in modern times that radios and cycles would be sold in the same outlet, but this was quite common in the 1940s and '50s. The lorry in the photograph is interesting. It was used to transport oxygen around the area, the double axles demonstrating just how heavy the pressurised tank must have been on the back of the sturdy vehicle.

Right: A crowded market scene recorded in the late 1950s, looking north along the High Street. A rare view of Blacketts department store is given by the picture, seen here on the immediate right of the view. There were three large department stores at the time this picture was taken - Robinsons Coliseum, Doggarts and Blacketts. Blacketts had formerly been D.Hill Carter & Co. Ltd before Blacketts

took over, and later the business was acquired by Waring and Gillow. Robinsons Coliseum eventually became Debenhams.

We shouldn't move on without mentioning the open-market traders, seen here with business in full swing. Market trading dates back around 700 years and has succeeded in attracting enough shoppers to the High Street to enable it to support the large stores already mentioned. The High Street began life as a residential area and became retail oriented later in its development. Of course, there was resistance to this from the residents of the street as the changeover took place, just as there was resistance from small retailers when the new developments came into town in the late 1960s and 1970s. Currently the debate is all about the effect that 'out of town' retail parks are having on the town centre's retail outlets. Perhaps, one day, we shall see our town centre's return to the residential function they performed over a century ago .

The centre of this photograph is dominated by the Vane Arms Hotel. Around 200 years ago the establishment played an important role in supporting the busy coaching route between the growing towns on the east coast. The picture was taken in November 1968 and shows the premises of some other well-known Stockton businesses including Laesers, United Friendly Insurance Company, Masterman's and, on the right of this picture, the lost and much lamented Black Lion Inn. All this property was, sadly, swept away in order to clear a site for the construction of the Castle Centre

development in the late 1960s. In the foreground the bus stand for services for Billingham and Hartlepool can be seen. 1968 was a dramatic year in terms of news on the world stage. In the USA Martin Luther King was assassinated in April, a tragedy followed just two months later by the assassination of Senator Robert Kennedy in California. Nearer to home, the first decimal coins appeared in Britain and London Bridge was sold to an American oil company.

Above: The impressive facade of Stockton's Co-Operative store is featured in this photograph which was taken in July 1969. Co-operative retailing began in Stockton in 1866 and the foundation stone for the premises at Wellington Street was laid just three years later. The store began trading in ernest on January 1st 1870. The store at Wellington was greatly upgraded and improved in the early 1930s, and the distinctive appearance we recognise today was created at that time. Over the years the Co-operative movement has gone from strength to strength, becoming involved in virtually every aspect of food production, processing and retailing for the benefit of its members, as well as other less obvious aspects of our daily lives ranging from banking, travel and furnishing to pharmacy and funeral services.

As a point of interest, this picture was taken less than two weeks before Neil Armstrong became the first human to walk on the moon. 1969 was a remarkable year for achievements. It saw the first flight of Concorde and the Jumbo Jet, as well as the maiden voyage of the liner QE2. ITV began making their first colour transmissions in the UK and the first Open University courses were offered by the BBC.

Below: There have been many varied and interesting shops along the High Street in Stockton, but the claim to be the smallest of these must surely rest with *Boncelle Tobaccos* owned by W.W Inglis Ltd. The smallest shop was also the shop which 'never had a customer inside it' - a boast which would surely be a cause for dismay for virtually every other retailer you could imagine. Furthermore, the shop could not even claim to have its own number on the street, though that didn't prevent it doing a brisk trade in all manner of smokers' requisites and sweets. According to local newspaper reports in 1966 the shop manageress Mrs. Norma Devereux of Acklam had worked behind the tiny counter for 20 years. The property was leased from the dry cleaning shop next door owned by James Smith and Sons, with whom a civilised agreement for the use of toilet facilities and the supply of refreshing cups of tea existed.

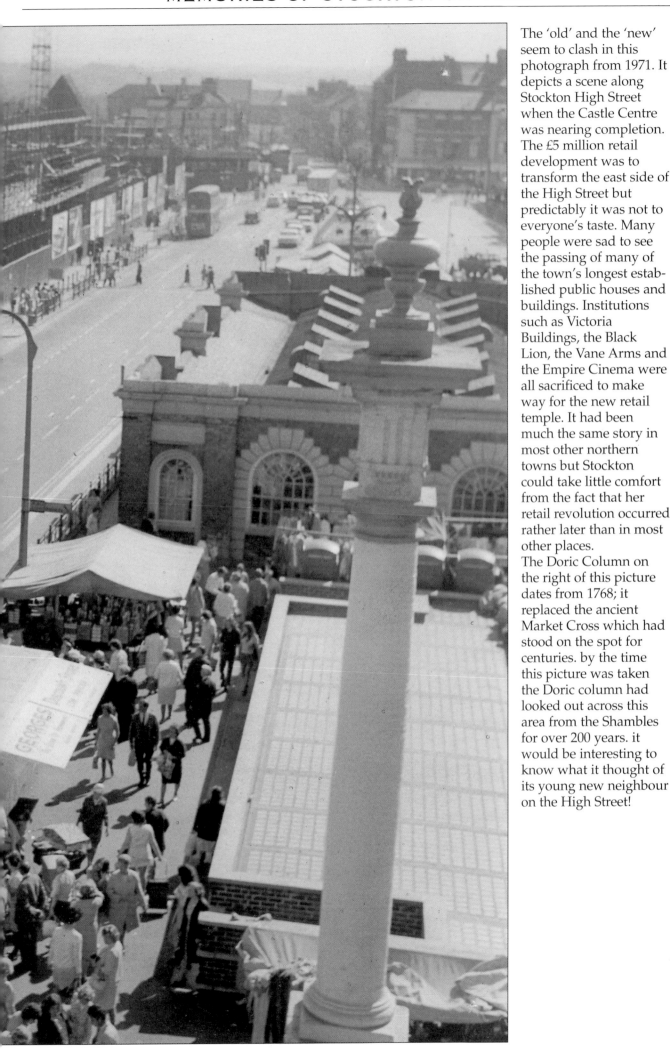

The 'old' and the 'new' seem to clash in this photograph from 1971. It depicts a scene along Stockton High Street when the Castle Centre was nearing completion. The £5 million retail development was to transform the east side of the High Street but predictably it was not to everyone's taste. Many people were sad to see the passing of many of the town's longest established public houses and buildings. Institutions such as Victoria Buildings, the Black Lion, the Vane Arms and the Empire Cinema were all sacrificed to make way for the new retail temple. It had been much the same story in most other northern towns but Stockton could take little comfort from the fact that her retail revolution occurred rather later than in most other places.

The Doric Column on the right of this picture dates from 1768; it replaced the ancient Market Cross which had stood on the spot for centuries. by the time this picture was taken the Doric column had looked out across this area from the Shambles for over 200 years. it would be interesting to know what it thought of its young new neighbour on the High Street!

This photograph of Victoria Buildings dates from the just before the time in 1964 when the structure was demolished. It shows to good effect the stylish and unusual facade which managed to set the property apart from the majority of functional but dull retail and office blocks on the high streets of many neighbouring towns. Keen eyes will just be able to make out the signs in most of the windows of the shops shown here; they were obviously announcing the imminent closure of the businesses concerned, and in some cases informing the public that trade would be transferred to another address. Some of the shops shown here are Carswell's, Northern Goldsmiths, Zip Cleaners, E. Ainsley White and F & F Mowbray Ltd. People may remember some other businesses which operated here even further in the past: Lilyan and Betty the hairdressers, Willman and Douglas Estate Agents, The Leeds Permanent Building Society, the Globe Boot Company, the Provident Clothing and Supply Company, and A. Hyams and Sons, house furnishers. It really was a sad day for Stockton when this fine old building was pulled down.

> "IT REALLY WAS A SAD DAY FOR STOCKTON WHEN THIS FINE OLD BUILDING WAS PULLED DOWN."

Events & occasions

Ted Lune is seen here with the proprietor of Duncan's the Tailors and a crowd of appreciative fans. Ted looks as if he has just cut through a high voltage cable, but in actual fact this was merely the symbolic ribbon across the entrance to the new tailors' shop, and the shocked expression simply an element of the comic art. The little lad in the gabardine coat is enjoying the occasion despite the fact that the comedian has temporarily pinched his school cap. The two Police Officers in the background look determined to make sure that the comic capers don't get out of hand. Happy Days!

Below: A moment was taken during this ceremony in the Town Hall to pose for a photograph to record the event. The picture dates from 1921 and shows the Prime Minister of New Zealand Mr. R. H Massey being granted the Freedom of the Borough of Stockton on Tees. The whole occasion looks very sombre and dignified, and the Union Flags against the walls in the background provide an impressive backdrop for the New Zealand flag and the smartly dressed civic officials. The picture was taken just two years before Stockton's most famous M.P first took his seat in Parliament to represent the Stockton constituency. This man was, of course, the great Harold McMillan, the man who went on to be Prime Minister in 1957 and 1959. Later, on entering the House of Lords and at the age of 90, McMillan took the title *Earl of Stockton* much to the delight of the local people he had at times represented during his long Parliamentary career. The Stockton-on-Tees constituency was divided into two separate constituencies in 1982. 'Stockton South' consisted of parts of Stockton along with Eaglescliffe, Yarm and Thornaby, while 'Stockton North' consisted of Billingham and the bulk of Stockton itself. Other events from 1921 include the establishment of the *British Broadcasting Corporation* ...and the death of a German-born composer, the original *Engelbert Humperdinck.*

Above: The Mayor and Mayoress of Stockton are seen taking the salute on a dais on the High Street in the mid 1960s. Two police officers and the mace bearer are pictured in front of the civic dignitaries and a mounted police officer adds to the sense of occasion created by the ceremony. The procession approaching the platform includes a number of firemen, girl guides and boy scouts, all smartly turned out as they pass the Union flag. At the time this picture was taken several well-known shops and businesses were trading from this end of town - among them Carrs, the Abbey National, Grantham's carpets and furniture showroom, and the Bradford and Bingley Building Society.

Right and below: 1977 will be remembered by 'royal-watchers' for Silver Jubilee of Her Majesty Queen Elizabeth II. The people of Stockton were honoured to learn that Her Majesty was to visit the town, as part of a tour of the north east, in July of that year. The tour began as the Royal Yacht Britannia sailed into Teesside, watched by thousands of well wishers. The Queen, accompanied by the Duke of Edinburgh, opened a new Tees Dock quay before moving on to visit the Prissick Base. After a visit to Durham the royal party went to Hartlepool where a new lifeboat was named. Throughout the tour the royal couple was accompanied by the Lord Lieutenant of Cleveland, Major Cecil Crossthwaite, along roads lined with thousands of flag-waving children adults and supporters of all ages.

In Stockton people began to arrive in the town centre a full five hours before the Queen was due to arrive. The area was alive with activity; Council officials and staff clearing every last piece of litter and making sure that everything was in place for the big moment. Security staff and police officers making final checks to ensure the safety and security of the VIPs. There was a carnival atmosphere in the town, encouraged by the enthusiastic playing of the Billingham Solar Band and renditions of 'Viva Espania' to the delight of the onlookers. Overhead, cloudy skies threatened rain, but somehow this didn't prey on the minds of the swelling crowds too much. the High Street was filling up, most of the people lining the edge of the pavement around the Town Hall and along the street towards the Parish Church. People took advantage of every available square foot of elevated space to which they could gain access. Every window-sill, balconies, high walls and rooftops. Every attempt was made to get an 'extra special' view of the visit. There were several false alarms, but when the leading police car appeared in view a satisfied hum, then deafening cheering grew from the crowd. This became even louder as the gleaming, glass-roofed limousine glided to a standstill on the High Street. Cameras flashed and their were gasps of appreciation as the Queen and Duke of Edinburgh climbed out of the stately vehicle. A small, open-space was already cordoned off for the initial introductions which were to take place before the eager crowd. As the Queen looked around she smiled and waved her appreciation for

the warmth of the Stockton welcome - to be met by even louder cheering and the waving of small red, white and blue flags. The introductions followed. The Lord Lieutenant presenting the Mayor, Councillor Lawrie Wild and his wife Mrs. Ethel Wild. The mayor's Chaplain, the Rev. Neville James, and the Stockton M.P and Transport Secretary Mr. Bill Rodgers. A special word was reserved for Stockton's hero, Victoria Cross holder Major Edward Cooper, and a posy of flowers was presented by Miss Susan Laskey, a student nurse at the North Tees General Hospital.

Shopping spree

The party moved inside the town Hall and the Queen was presented with a bound copy of Brewster's *History of Stockton*, and performed the honour of unveiling a plaque on the north wall of the building, next to the one she unveiled on her 1956 visit. Cheers followed as the royal party came out of the Town Hall and back onto the High Street. A brief walkabout then took place, with the Queen and Duke of Edinburgh chatting to the people of Stockton in a friendly, relaxed manner. From here it was back to the Royal Yacht and Tees Dock.

During the visit hundreds of floral tributes had been handed to the royal party and these were collected and saved. At the end of the visit there were enough flowers to fill two cars, and these were shared between Middlesborough General Hospital and Stockton's North Tees General Hospital. A simple note from the Queen's Equery read "I hope your patients enjoy these."

On the evening before their departure the Queen and Duke of Edinburgh entertained local dignitaries aboard Britannia. Outside on the quayside there were chants from waiting crowds who were rewarded by an appearance on deck of the royal couple. Later, the Royal Marines 'beat the retreat' much to the delight

of the guests and onlookers, and another appearance on deck by the Queen and the Duke at around midnight, signalled the end of a successful and enjoyable visit to the area. In all it was estimated that around 250,000 people had turned out to express their support, and the Assistant Chief Constable of Cleveland paid tribute to the exemplary behaviour of the crowds throughout the tour. It was not until the early hours of the morning that Britannia set sail for Tyneside, silently passing South Gare at 4.30 am.

Above: Several clues combine to give us the impression that this picture dates from the mid to late 1930s. The period motorcar is an obvious example, as is the clothing worn by the shoppers in the scene. The cobbles and the road markings are typical of the time and the heavily-shaded windows of the retail premises in the picture suggest that it was taken during the summer months. The Royal Exchange Hotel can be seen on the left of the picture. It served the needs of many thirsty Stockton drinkers up until it closed in 1941. The 'Neville' store beside it was a boot and shoe retailer. Stewart's clothiers operated their business from Tees House until the dawn of the 1970s and boasted branches in London and Aberdeen.

An unusual view of the High Street recorded in the late 1950s, with the Town Hall in the centre-distance. The (eight-foot diameter) clock on the Town Hall is showing 10.50 am and the market traders along the centre of the High Street appear to be doing a brisk trade. On the right of the picture Marks and Spencers store stands next to the Weaver to Wearer discount gentlemens' tailors - they had scores of branches throughout the north. Building work was underway on the plot on the other side of Marks and Spencers as the new Littlewoods store took shape. Victoria Buildings dominates the left of the picture, the premises of Willman and Douglas and Northern Goldsmiths can be seen, with The Welcut Tailors Ltd shop occupying the corner position on the block.

Behind Victoria Buildings, at roof top level, it is just possible to make out the lettering on the wall of the Blacketts department store. The quality of this picture is exceptional and gives an interesting insight into a typical 1950s day on Stockton High Street.

Above: A mid 1960s view across the stalls in the direction of the Town Hall. Stockton's unusual former seat of local government has seen all kinds of uses in its long history, including a lock-up cell for local offenders, a public house and a function room. The Town House was rebuilt upon a site occupied by an earlier structure in 1735. The clock tower which gives it the distinctive appearance we have become accustomed to, was added soon afterwards, in 1744, when an extension was built making it possible to site four small retail shops within the building.

Right: This close up view of the Market Cross was captured in 1967. The structure dates from 1768 - a remarkable 21 years before the French Revolution sent shock waves around the governments of every European nation. This picture is taken looking in the direction of the southern end of the High Street with the Shambles in the foreground. This was the location of 'The Hirings,' the event which took place in May and November in which prospective employees would gather in the hope of being selected by farmers and landowners for fixed-term contracts. On choosing an employee the farmer would 'seal' the deal with a half crown (or a shilling depending on which historical records you take notice of) - the coin becoming known as 'God's Penny.' The event developed into something resembling a fair. Many attractions would be present, including Boxing Booths, John Jarley's Waxworks and even, occasionally, Madame Tussauds' Waxworks. The Hirings took place for many years up until the First World War. After this time, however they began to lessen in popularity to the extent to which they were no longer viable. The Shambles - a name which originates from one meaning 'a place to buy meat or fish' - centred around a building which was built in 1825 at a cost of £1960. It replaced an earlier structure which dated from the late 1600s. On the right of the picture Stewarts clothing shop is in view, dwarfing the Radio Rentals shop below it.

Left: This is a publicity photograph from October 1960. More mature readers may recognise the characteristic blank expression on the face of the personality shown here - it is the unmistakable hallmark of Ted Lune. In the fairly early days of television Ted Lune managed, for a time at least, to make the transition from the music hall to the small screen. He was popular with all ages but had a special rapport with young people. The reason for his visit to Stockton was to open the new branch of Duncan's the Tailors. He is seen here looking like a startled rabbit as bemused stage-struck tailors attempt to 'measure up' to him.

Below: This picture dates from 1961 and features four businesses which were located along the High Street at the time. Just in view on the left is the National and Provincial Bank, with the Bank Chambers above. *Number 125*, next door, was occupied by Charles Morris, the shop known 'for its finer furniture.' Althams sold a variety of fancy goods and other products in shops in towns and cities throughout the north of England. At one time, in the early years of their existence, they were tea dealers, and the company still operates today in many towns as a respected travel agency firm. Maypole Dairies occupied number 127 High Street and the shop next door became a paint and wallpaper retailer after a long spell as Brown's the shoe retailers.

Above: An exterior view of Leslie Brown's toy and record shop, dating, most probably from the end of the 1950s. The large sign for 'His Masters Voice' a dominant record label of the day would have attracted the record buying public towards the shop. The introduction of the 'single' vinyl record, the weekly popular music charts and transistor radios resulted in a growth in the popularity of music records among young people, and this was welcome news for the growing number of high street record retailers. We can guess that this photograph was taken in October or very early November as space in Brown's window has been devoted to a display of *Standard* fireworks. Yet another Stockton gents' outfitters can be seen next door to Browns; Bradleys were having a sale when this picture was taken - shirts can be seen for the bargain price of £1 each. This was the place that buses operated by United Bus Company Ltd. would stop on some of their longer routes. Whitby, Scarborough, Bridlington were some of the east coast destinations, but there were services to places as far away Liverpool, Doncaster and even London.

Below: The interior of Brown's toy shop's model railway department. Here hundreds of local boys would drool over the latest *Hornby* sets and the very detailed layouts which characterised the centre of the shop and ensured its popularity with rail enthusiasts of all ages. Some of the publications displayed in the shop would have made compelling reading for visitors to the department. They include *Model Railway News* and the more obscure *British Locomotive Shed Directory*.

A small section of the shop was put aside for sales of chemistry sets, again, mainly the province of little lads - and their dads. This picture was taken in a rare quiet period before the rush which accompanied the weeks leading up to Christmas. Under normal circumstances, and particularly on Saturdays, you could hardly move in the shop for miniature rail enthusiasts and their parents.

Children would gasp in wonder on entering Leslie Brown's toy shop. And no wonder, considering the range of exciting toys shown in this picture. An understandable first reaction is to think just how much toys have changed over the last thirty years ago, but studying the photograph in more detail makes one realise that many have remained popular to this day. The cycles are a good example - we probably all remember our first three-wheeler... and then the next precarious step on to two wheels. some of the bikes shown here would have been the object of many small boys' and girls' dreams, longed for in the weeks running up to Christmas Day. The Scalextric sets are another example of toys which are still popular. A smaller set, the VIP Model Roadway, by a different manufacturer is offered here for £8 19s 6d. Pedal cars and ride-on toy trucks (priced from £2 9s 11d) can be seen in the picture, along with mini-table tennis sets for just under £4, and those small toy pianos that virtually every child seemed to have at one time.

Rows of canvas-topped stalls stand on the narrow central area of the High Street where cars would park on other days. The Wednesday and Saturday market days have attracted thousands of bargain hunters and eager shoppers to the High Street and to surrounding shops for hundreds of years. They arrive, not just from the Stockton area, but from many towns throughout the north east - and beyond. Many of the stallholders have been loyal to Stockton's open market for several generations. A broad spectrum of products is represented on the stalls, from food and clothing to household and electrical goods - with everything in between. At one time there was a cattle market and the associated agricultural goods market combined to form an important aspect of market trading in the town. Stockton was once a leading corn trader and supplier. Cattle trading ended in the late 1950s and the site of the old cattle market, known as the Square, is now covered by the Central Library. Some familiar high street names can be seen in this picture, including Freeman Hardy Willis, True Form and Boots. The picture was taken in 1973, the year which saw Britain become a full member of the EEC, the introduction of VAT and the Senate Hearings on the Watergate scandal begin in the USA.

Above: An interior view of the *Chain Library Shop* which dates from the 1960s. The 'library' element of the business was situated at the rear of the shop, while many other fast-moving lines can be seen lining the extensive shelving in this picture. Some of the items are bound to bring back memories; the cowboy outfits, reflecting the popularity of television cowboy programmes at the time, the vast array of plastic cars and other toys demonstrating the growing use of plastic in toy manufacturing which led to a wider range of cheaper toys for children. Various annuals were sold here, many, as now, relating to the favourite comic books of our youth. Finally, much shelf space is devoted here to the display and ultimate sale of greetings cards. Most of us in the 'sixties would have bought birthday cards and Christmas cards - but it is amazing to consider just how many excuses the card manufacturers have found in more recent times to sell us cards for all occasions.

Bird's eye view

A view of Stockton which few people will have had the opportunity to see before. The picture was taken from an aircraft by a Bradford company which was well known for this kind of work. It dates from 1954 and shows a sea of terraced property tightly packed around the 'hinterland' of the town of Stockton. The characteristic tight curve of the River Tees can be seen at the top of the photograph with the High Street and industrial area beside the quayside beyond it. This view has seen radical changes since the picture was taken - in common with similar-sized towns in the north the tendency has been for residential areas to move into the outskirts of the town and for larger numbers of terraced properties to be replaced by modern, better equipped council-owned housing. Ring roads have eased the town centre congestion which made even short local journeys frustrating, and large, cleared areas in the town centre turned over to car parking. Old industrial sites have been cleared and the land put to use as modern retail or business parks, and even high quality residential developments.

"..STOCKTON HIGH STREET APPEARS TO CUT A SWATHE THROUGH THE BUILT-UP AREA OF THE TOWN CENTRE.."

The long, broad path of Stockton High Street appears to cut a swathe through the built up area of the town centre, beside the more natural feature formed by the River Tees. Market stalls, the Town Hall, the Shambles and Victoria Buildings can all be recognised in this picture which was taken from on-board an aircraft flying at 1000 feet above the area. The picture was taken in September 1954. It is interesting to see the evidence of Stockton's activities as a port - the large quayside cranes and adjacent railway sidings and warehouses giving the game away. The aerial view shows just how haphazard the layout of the town centre was during the 1950s, before the planners really began to organise things in a more co-ordinated manner. In the year this photograph was taken Roger Bannister ran the first four minute mile and, at long last, all rationing in Britain finally ended after its introduction during the war.

An aerial view of Stockton which highlights the close proximity of the River Tees to the new shopping developments alongside the High Street. The large square outline of the Swallow Hotel can be seen at the right of the new Castle Centre, Stockton's boldest step into the new age of sophisticated retailing. Work had started on the major £5m development on the east side of the High Street in June 1970. Over the years efforts have been made to maintain Stockton's leading position as a retail

centre, drawing shoppers from a wide area into the town. In more recent times many smaller shops have sprung up in restored properties adjacent to the High Street. Moves have been made to limit the areas where motors are allowed access so that a safer, healthier and generally more pleasant shopping environment is formed. In this picture, hundreds of motorcars can be seen parked in the middle of the Stockton's main street. The photograph dates from the early 1970s.

At work

> ## "IT WAS A SAD DAY FOR STOCKTON WHEN THE EMPIRE CINEMA WAS PULLED DOWN.."

It was a sad day for Stockton when the Empire Cinema was pulled down in the late 1960s. Here we see two demolition men grasping one of the letters which made up the word EMPIRE CINEMA in a photograph from January 1969. On the right is the Royal Hotel and the 'bus passing them on the High Street advertises vacancies for conductors. The popular entertainment venue stood on the corner of Castlegate and the High Street. It began life in 1908 as the Castle Theatre and was an imposing building designed to Edwardian style complete with interior *Italianate* painted ceilings, fountains and palm trees. As was the case with many similar establishments a change to 'cinema' was made when the lure of live entertainment could no longer fill the seats. Billiards was a popular pass-time and it was catered for by the Empire until its closure, which was briefly preceded by a spell as a bingo hall. The site formerly occupied by this grand old lady of the entertainment world is now the location of a major hotel.

Left: A small crowd gathered to watch a team of professional removers from K. W Devereux and Sons as they gently guided this piano out of the first floor window of the Alma Hotel on Dovecote Street. The picture was taken in the late 1950s and the landlord at the time was Eric Brigham. It would be unusual to see a similar sight today, as the practice of using a small crane on window-ledges is outlawed by modern insurance companies. Apparently some modern buildings are not constructed as robustly as those of yesteryear!

Guiding the piano from out on the ledge was the Devereux foreman, the late Wilfy Hall, and leaning on the window ledge is the founder of the firm Ken Devereux. Waiting anxiously on the ground was the late Clifford "Chippy"Almond.

Below: An almost desolate view along High Street, with several names from the past lying between the Town Hall on the right and the Regal Cinema (No, 90) on the left. Moving along the street, some of the names included Mrs. King's Refreshment Rooms, Martins Bank, A.Wright and Company, outfitters, The Home and Colonial Stores (grocers), the Victoria Inn, Meadow Dairies and the Stockton 'Cinema.' Notice that the road at this time was still cobbled.

The Regal dates back as far as April 1935 and was a purpose-built cinema from that time. The company was absorbed into the *Odeon* group of cinemas and the building shown here was eventually pulled down in the mid-'60s in order to erect a more modern facility on the same site. This, sadly, was not enough to preserve the building's use as a cinema and the premises became a nightclub some years later.

Below: Five tough-looking tipper trucks are seen here in a Stockton garage workshop, receiving attention before being used on a local road building scheme. The Leyland truck in the foreground was registered in 1965 and was probably around seven years old when this picture was taken. The Scammel trucks, by comparison look almost brand new and show markings which indicate that they were owned by the *Tarmac* group of companies.

"THE LAST VESSEL TO VISIT THE PORT IN AN OFFICIAL CAPACITY WAS HMS LEWISTON"

Stockton's had a long history as a thriving port, but this ended in 1967. The last vessel to visit the port in an official capacity was HMS Lewiston. Stockton's importance as a port was linked to its association with the export of corn and coal. Shipbuilding had been an important commercial pursuit here, but was prone to the ups and downs of the economic cycles which had such a drastic effect on the fortunes of shipyards throughout the world. The decline had set in as far back as the second half of the last century but the slumps of the early 1920s and early '30s caused the remaining yards- and the men employed within them - to suffer very badly. This picture dates from 1957 and features the Stella Mary registered at Stockton.

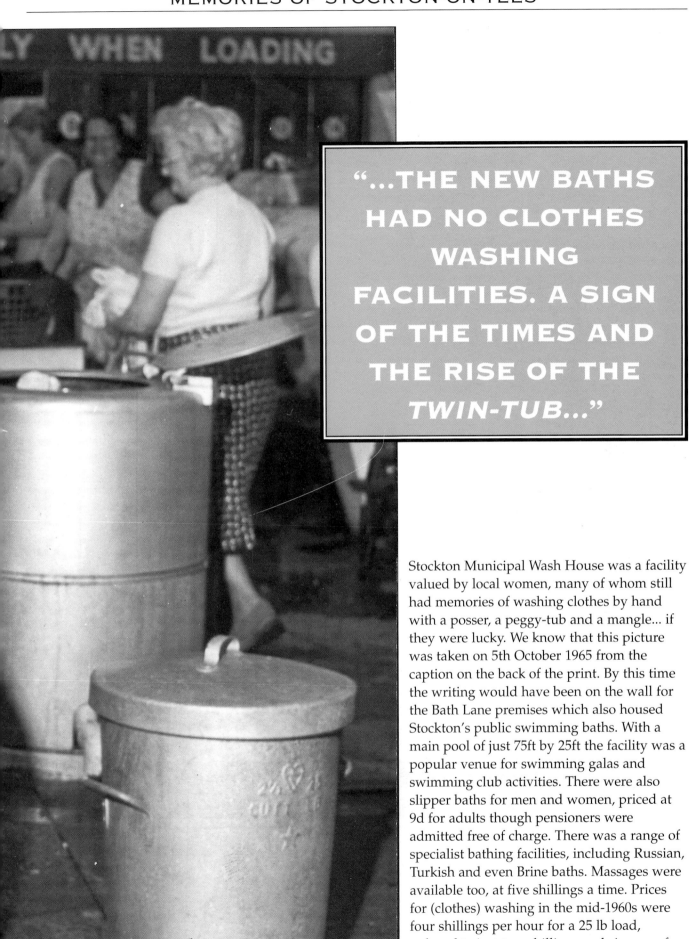

"...THE NEW BATHS HAD NO CLOTHES WASHING FACILITIES. A SIGN OF THE TIMES AND THE RISE OF THE *TWIN-TUB*..."

Stockton Municipal Wash House was a facility valued by local women, many of whom still had memories of washing clothes by hand with a posser, a peggy-tub and a mangle... if they were lucky. We know that this picture was taken on 5th October 1965 from the caption on the back of the print. By this time the writing would have been on the wall for the Bath Lane premises which also housed Stockton's public swimming baths. With a main pool of just 75ft by 25ft the facility was a popular venue for swimming galas and swimming club activities. There were also slipper baths for men and women, priced at 9d for adults though pensioners were admitted free of charge. There was a range of specialist bathing facilities, including Russian, Turkish and even Brine baths. Massages were available too, at five shillings a time. Prices for (clothes) washing in the mid-1960s were four shillings per hour for a 25 lb load, reduced to just two shillings and sixpence for OAPs. The new baths a short distance away on Church Road would have no clothes washing facilities when they opened, a sign of the times ...and the rise of the *twin-tub*.

A close-up view of the serving hatch and narrow counter of Stockton's smallest shop. The business was open between the hours of 8.30 and 6.00pm and was well supported by a loyal band of customers. A sign in the window advertises Wee Willem Cigars for 5s 6d (27.5p). The manageress is pictured here posing for the camera.

Four lovely young ladies pose for the photographer on the roof of the Littlewoods store on the High Street in this 1970s picture. Retailing has served to provide thousands of employment opportunities for Stockton people over the years and these girls appear to be just starting out in the world of work. The wall belonging to Marks and Spencer's store 'next door' can be seen on the left, and the Royal Oak public house is visible in the background, across the tops of the market stalls.

Right: These ladies were tasked with an important job in the finishing department of Rembrant Ltd., the respected Stockton ladies wear manufacturers. It must have been hard work at times, pressing and ironing all the dresses manufactured by their colleagues in the rest of the factory. The business had been in existence for decades, though not always at this location on Maritime Road, near Church Road. Before the move to Maritime Road the firm occupied a mill site around 200 yards away. Around 250 people worked in the business and there was a widespread sense of sadness when a downturn in demand caused the business to close.

Below: In October 1971 Stockton entered the age of concrete and consumerism by opening its first roof top car park. This was a time of great change in the world of retailing and Stockton High Street's eastern side would be changed forever with the erection of the controversial Castle Centre. The new shopping centre managed to attract 5 large stores and had 50 shop units to accompany with the covered hall and 120-bedroomed hotel. The multi-storey car park had a capacity of over 1000 vehicles. Stockton has come a long way since the opening of her first roof-top car park around 30 years ago. An impressive new University College and several high-tech industries add to the impression that Stockton is a modern go-ahead town with a bright future.

Problem castings, no problem

On a July day in 1947, Tom Wolverson, founder of The Stockton Casting Company Ltd. and the Mayor of Stockton watched a plaque being cast with the first metal melted at the opening of a new foundry in Ross Road, Stockton. The Mayor of Stockton later received the plaque that had been made to mark the first business established on a green field site which was meant to be named Foundry Road. The name was changed in appreciation of support for the project received from Alderman Ross. The original foundry was constructed from second hand bricks and timber from a demolished Whessoe building in Darlington. Metallurgist, Tom Wolverson, had trained at Wolverhampton Technical College where he is remembered as being a *Grade A* student throughout his stay. In fact, Tom went on to teach at the College, before coming north, first to work in Leeds, then to Stockton. The company began trading as a small, privately-owned jobbing foundry producing grey iron castings by Cupola melting. In other words, pig or cast-iron was melted in furnaces lined with firebricks and gannister. A cupola is an upright, cylindrical metal structure. Metal, coke, alloys and limestone were charged down through the top and air was blown in near the bottom causing the coke to fire, thus melting the metal. He was known as 'Ten Thou Tom' because of his obsession with accuracy. He was well known too for his adage, 'Problem castings, no problem'. The principle behind this saying is still upheld by the management today.

There was a small workforce of six, two of whom had accompanied Tom from Leeds. Tom, his son

Robin and his wife Minnie worked together. Robin became a director in 1965 and prepared himself to take over when Tom should retire.

Robin and his wife Jean were good friends of Jet Harris of The Shadows.

Above: The July 1947 casting of a special plaque to mark the opening of Stockton Casting Company watched by the founder Tom Wolverson and the Mayor of Stockton. **Right:** *A plaque presented to The Stockton Casting Company denoting membership of the Institute of British Foundrymen*

A company minute book has been kept from the day the firm was founded so that there is a continuous record, meticulously kept of the company's progress since 1947.

Robin Wolverson takes over

Robin became managing director in 1977 and in that same year Malcolm Collins, the company's current sales director, joined the firm. Tom introduced the fleximelt system when the medium frequency electric furnaces were installed, which made the production of components in a wide variety of material specifications possible,

Diversifying in this way proved to be vital during the widespread contraction of the foundry industry. In the period 1978 to 1992, foundry work in the UK decreased by about fifty per cent. In this same period,

The Stockton Casting Company Ltd experienced continuous growth of 4% a year with later major expansions in 1980 and 1985.

The present managing director of Stockton Castings is Brian Killman. He enters the story in 1979 when Robin Wolverson met him in America on a tour of American foundries. Tom referred to this event as the 'porridge trip' because it was organised by Quaker Oats. After that there was no contact between the two men for seven years. Then Brian Killman, who was working as a foundry consultant, needed some castings sourcing and contacted Robin again. The firm Mr Killman was advising needed castings and had been let down by its regular supplier. The latter firm refused to release the patterns that would be needed if someone else was to make the castings. Brian Killman put on the drivers overalls and "liberated" the patterns and took them to The Stockton Casting Company Ltd who made the castings. They delivered them by Christmas, three months earlier than the regular supplier said it was possible.

Robin and Brian didn't meet again for over a year until, out of the blue, in 1987, Robin called Brian and invited him to an evening match at Middlesbrough

Above: An atmospheric picture showing molten metal being poured into a crucible. Left: A signed autograph of Jet Harris of the Shadows, a friend of Robin and Jean Wolverson.

where S.C.C were match sponsors and Robin and Jean's son was mascot. Naturally enough, the conversation turned to work and business in general. Sadly, Robin died only weeks later. Malcolm Collins, S & M Director today, took the helm, but Robin's death was a severe blow and these were hard times for the company, to such an extent that Jean felt the need to take a break. She took a flight to Australia with her two children and stayed there for a month. While in Australia Jean remembered that Robin had said that if she was ever in need of help or advice for the business she should contact Brian Killman. On her return from Australia she found that, by sheer coincidence, Malcolm Collins had contacted Brian to inform him of Robin's death. Malcolm offered Brian a job, which he refused, but offered to help on a part-time basis as an advisor and consultant. Here began the long recovery process. In due course romance developed between Brian and Jean, and Brian offered to take Jean into his own consultancy business. Jean's

commitment to The Stockton Casting Company, and to the Wolverson name would not allow her to do that. Consequently, for a number of years Brian continued to run his own foundry consultancy, but he would use his expertise on the manufacturing side to benefit The Stockton Casting Company.

In December 1988 Brian became a director and, as a consequence of his increased involvement with The Stockton Casting Company he withdrew from his consulting business over a period of time. His customers were, however, only too happy to bring their business to The Stockton Casting Company, confident in the knowledge of his reputation and reliability over many years. Brian was so confident in the company's prospects for recovery and growth that he invested a considerable amount of his own capital in the firm on becoming a director. This financial support was vital at the time.

To: THE STOCKTON CASTING COMPANY

Thank you for your help which is keeping the Battle of Britain Memorial Flight airworthy.

30 June '89.

Barry Sears.
Engineering Officer.

In 1980, when Tom and Minnie Wolverson retired, land was bought from Lonsdales Civil Engineering Company. The next year T W Turner's Pattern Shop was purchased and the pattern-making was taken to Ross Road four years later when The Stockton Casting Company bought Cockburns.

In 1990 Brian Killman became managing Director so that Malcolm Collins could concentrate on sales. A strategy so effective that Brian had to act quite quickly to acquire the old Tioxide land adjacent in order to commission a new foundry to honour his commitment to the workforce.

In the early nineties Tom and Minnie Wolverson died within a couple of years of each other.

More expansion.
The next significant expansion came in 1994. Melting capacity increased five-fold when two 850 kilowatt medium frequency furnaces were installed with a melting capability each of 1 tonne per fifty minutes. By now the company was one of only a few iron foundries left in the Stockton area. More land was acquired for further buildings, plant and machinery. The facilities comprised a foundry, a finishing area and a pattern shop. The foundry housed moulding work and coremaking. The latter process involves making intricate cores of specially prepared sand and placing them in a mould to provide a hole or cavity in a casting. Metal melting and pouring is also done in the foundry.

Construction and repair of pattern equipment in timber and epoxy resin takes place in the Pattern shop. Castings are produced using a variety of materials and the main products are Diesel Engine components such as exhaust manifolds, turbine housings, pressure cylinders and various general engineering components. Several of the major customers are high profile world class companies.

During this time, the foundations were laid to produce an even wider range of good quality, approved, high-integrity castings. These vary from one to fifteen hundred kilos in weight with quantities ranging from one-off to ten thousand a year.

The foundry has a high reputation for making castings to very precise demands including parts for large diesel engines, compressors, pumps and blowers. It successfully casts a very wide range of ferrous alloys, complying with all the relevant and recognised technical standards.

The company use high-tech computer based systems technically and commercially. At the same time a commitment to develop high quality assurance systems conforming to BS5750 part 2 was implemented. The company presently complies with ISO9002.

Top: Robin Wolverson is pictured fourth from the left at the John Stuart Research Laboratories of Quaker Oats Limited during the SO_2 study tour in America, 1981. This was the tour on which he met Brian Killman also pictured above. *Above:* The casting of these greyhounds, a familiar part of Stockton's street scene show how versatile the firm can be. *Left:* A painting of the Battle of Britain Memorial Flight presented to Stockton Casting as a thankyou for their help in maintaining the aircraft.

The Stockton Casting Company recognises that efficient administrative systems are vital to successful foundry activity and have invested heavily in tailored-for-the-job computer hardware, software and training in its proper and efficient use.

To celebrate all this, on its birthday, July 4th 1997, the company allowed itself the luxury of nostalgia by re-enacting that 1947 casting ceremony watched by the current Mayor of Stockton.

In July this year, fifty years on, the company is still at Ross Road. It can reflect on how far it has moved up the league since the early days. Even 20 years ago it employed only forty people, with a turnover of just £370,000. Today the Stockton Casting Company aims for a turnover of more than four million pounds and grey iron contributes only 10% of its manufacturing output. It takes nationwide orders for a wide variety of designs and materials, most of which are destined for export. The company has its own internet web site and is on e-mail, so that its customers can be contacted quickly and their orders dealt with speedily. It is working towards the rare UK automotive industry's quality standard of QS9000.

However, its achievements would not have been possible without the skills and co-operation of the 90 strong workforce. Demonstration of the firm's commitment to its employees has been its recent Teesside TEC's Investors in People Award.

A celebration. The new foundry was inaugurated on 4th July 1997 and is now fully operational.

Also attending this second ceremony, together with current directors and staff were some of the firm's main customers and suppliers.

The company, however, looks forward rather than back. It is still family-owned, the principal owners being Brian and Jean Killman. Mr Killman, the present managing director believes that success depends on continuous re-investment in the latest technology.

Top: A re-enactment of the 1947 casting to mark the 50th Anniversary of the company. Below: From left to right: Mrs Jean Killman, Mr Tony Gernon, Director of Enterprise and Economic Development Teesside TEC, Mr Brian Killman and Mr Malcolm Collins.

Above: This delightful scene was captured at the turn of the century. The clarity of the picture belies the fact that it is almost 100 years old. Note how clean and new Victoria Buildings appears, on the right of the picture, and the enormous gold lettering which forms the sign of the *Cash Clothing Company* a couple of blocks below it. There are so many interesting features in this scene that it is difficult to know where to start describing them. It is another example of a picture being better for the fact that the people featured in it are unaware of the photographer. Also, it is unusually sharp for the period - possibly as much by luck as good photographic skills. The variety of clothing worn by the people here is interesting - all manner of hats and dresses which typify these Edwardian times. We can tell from the shadows and the clock on the Parish Church that it was approaching mid-day. The weather looks hot - at least one lady is carrying an umbrella to shade herself from the sun. The cobblestones, the gas lamps and the electric trams add to the character and the atmosphere created by the photograph. It must rank as one of the best images portraying ordinary people on Stockton High Street at the turn of the century. We are grateful to Mr. Ian Sinclair for allowing us to use it in the book.

Giving a lift to industry

Born in 1826, Jonathan Pickering founded Pickerings Limited in 1854. By then he had invented and patented the original Pickering's Pulley Block with which he established his reputation, so that his company, one of the oldest engineering firms on Teesside, was soon well established.

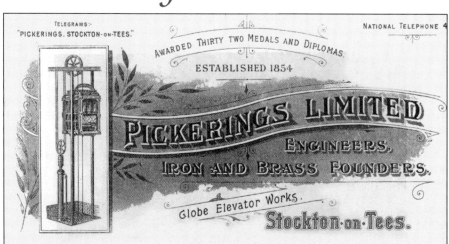

The pulley far surpassed other types in use and at the time it was much marvelled at. Mr Pickering's company at first concentrated exclusively on making these pulley blocks which found a ready market throughout the world.

As time went on further improvements in hoisting appliances were developed and the company successfully exhibited its products at Philadelphia, USA in 1876, at Bremen in Germany in 1874 and in Amsterdam in 1888. In each place they were awarded medals in recognition of the excellence and high quality of their goods. These medals were still in the possession of the company and much prized by them until they were stolen in 1972.

In 1887, in view of the rapidly expanding business the firm was incorporated as a limited liability company under the name and title of Pickerings Limited. It continued to make blocks, cranes and hoisting appliances.

Above: The firm's letterhead in the early years of the century. It reminds customers of the 32 medals and diplomas awarded to the company. *Below:* The electric lift erecting department in 1905. Electricity revolutionised lifting machinery at the turn of the century. The early electric lifts had three safety gears to prevent accident so that the car would stop even if the lift rope broke.

Pickerings Limited was one of the first firms in the country to start making lifts. They invented the self-sustaining hand lift and service lift and developers of the belt power and hydraulic lift

In 1888 they designed and manufactured their first electric lift which was installed at the Middlesbrough Co-operative Society. The first fully automatic push button lift was made in 1896. It was in those days a considerable achievement and was the forerunner of many developments in the lift industry.

Meanwhile, in 1891, after the death of Jonathan Pickering, the Board of Directors invited Mr John Fothergill to become the next Managing Director. Mr Fothergill was at that time an independent marine engineering consultant who had advised Pickerings in the past on matters of ship docking and unloading systems. He accepted and now five generations of his family have owned and managed the firm.

Between 1854 and 1900 the company designed and built several streets of terraced houses surrounding the factory premises to house both workers and supervisors.

With such a background of experience it is hardly surprising that Pickerings has become one of the leading lift manufacturers in the country, then, as now their facilities were developing using all the most up-to-date technologies.

Above: A self-landing hoist. These were made in various sizes and were a convenient arrangement where it was not possible to install a lift. They would unload goods directly from a cart and transport them to any floor of a building. They were useful in canal work and for unloading trucks.
Right: A corner of the pulley block fitting department in 1905. The pulley block was the invention of Jonathan Pickering, the company's founder.

Pickerings' contribution to the War Effort 1939-45
In the twelve months before the war, the company had a record output of three hundred lifts. Among these were, for the time, modern high-speed lifts with power operated doors and all the most up-to-date methods, again for the time, of control. This was in addition to other standard lines of hoisting equipment. When war broke out, practically all commercial building work was suspended and suitable work had to be found for the company's men and equipment.

The first contracts directly connected with the war were for the manufacture of all types of handling equipment for the production of aluminium for aircraft. Entirely new methods of production on a tremendous scale were required and Pickerings were entrusted with the complete design and manufacture of handling plant for heat treatment furnaces in a number of the largest aluminium factories in the country.

Many machines were designed and supplied, including those for the manufacture of Rolls Royce aircraft engines, airscrews, bombs, armour plate and large gun-barrel forgings.

During this period, manufacture of electric lifts continued in small quantities for essential indus-

trial and war purposes. Among a number of interesting facilities installed were the ammunition lifts for the cross-channel guns on the south coast, and over a hundred food lifts for various aerodromes.

In spite of the big change over in production, capacity was also found for the manufacture of Trench Mortars. From 1940 onwards, one department was working day and night to satisfy the almost insatiable demand for these weapons.

In 1941 the demand for various kinds of equipment grew so heavy that it was necessary to increase the size of the works. A new shop was built of approximately ten thousand square feet and new plant was installed. This enabled the company to take on extra work and production of various parts of Bailey Bridge and floating Pontoon Bridge, was undertaken and continued until the end of the war.

Amongst the war time difficulties encountered, not the least was the call up of over 30% of the firm's pre-war employees. Much extra responsibility fell on the remaining old hands who, amongst other duties, trained many new ones.

The barrage balloons used during the second war contained a number of design features from the first Kite Balloon Winches that were designed and built by Pickerings during the 1914-18 war.

When the war was over a voluntary Soldiers' Fund was set up to help members in the services.

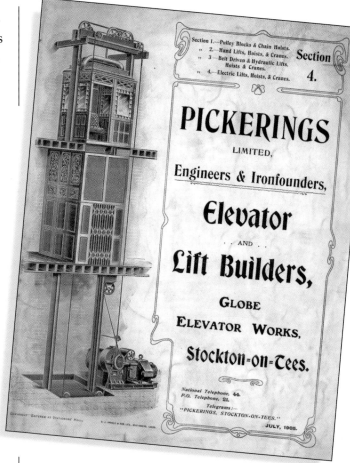

After the war, Pickering lifts were bought chiefly for large office buildings and department stores but automatic lifts were supplied for large blocks of flats and all kinds of industries. The firm sold to many well known passenger ship companies and oil tanker fitters.

However, lifts were not the company's only products. It continued to specialise in many forms of handling plant and furnace charging machines. An efficient sales and service organisation was an essential feature of the company's business and self-contained, fully staffed branches for this purpose were established throughout the country.

Above: Section four of the July 1905 catalogue showing one of the lifts available from the Globe Elevator Works. *Left:* A freight vehicle lift used by the express parcel delivery firm, Carter Paterson.

throughout the world to countries including Russia, China, India, Brazil, Iceland and most European countries.

By a happy coincidence, the centenary of the company coincided with fifty years' service of its then chairman, Mr John Fothergill who had joined the company in 1904. The company had at that time another three employees who had served for half a century and there was much to celebrate. Not least was the fact that, during the whole of their existence, Pickerings had given almost continuous employment to their men. Even in the disastrous thirties only a brief spell of short time was worked, whilst, among rival firms in the

In spite of the large demand for lifts at home, the export market had not been neglected and lifts were being supplied

Above: A photograph from the thirties of a Pickerings service van.
Top: A mooring mast for the airships of the Empire Airship Service. The mooring masts were provided with Pickerings Passenger lifts to carry passengers up to the airships.
Right: A railway station installation which combines lever and push button control. It was delivered for service in 1919.

A picture from the Admiralty Book of a field power unit used during WWI, as manufactured by Pickerings.

district, one after another was going out of existence. A centenary celebration dinner was held at the Zetland Hotel, Saltburn with Chairman, John Fothergill as toastmaster.

Pickerings Lifts Europe
Under its present title the company is completely independent and privately owned. It has been at the forefront of the lift industry now for over 140 years. To ensure that they remain at the cutting edge of lift technology and market requirements Pickerings' managers have created a sophisticated

Left: *During the Second World War the usual activities of the company were suspended so that Pickerings could manufacture field mortars for the war effort.*

since the company believes dialogue is the key to a successful project. The range of products currently includes passenger lifts, freight lifts, service lifts, panoramic lifts and bed passenger lifts. There is a modernisation division and a customer support service division.

The company has achieved accreditation to ISO 9001 with a scope which covers design, engineering, manufacture, supply, installation, modernisation, repair and maintenance of its lifts and lift equipment. The accreditation covers not only their integrated design and production facilities but also all their regional offices and the activities of their engineers on site.

network with other companies and suppliers across the European Community. To help with clear communications they are linked to them via their computer network. This is important

Above: The manufacturing plant in Stockton.
Top: The liner, The Himalaya, one of many ocean going liners fitted with lifts from Pickerings.
Right: The new Group facilities in the Netherlands.

Harkers Engineering - Fred Harker's unadulterated nostalgia

In 1878 Francis Todd Harker founded the family business, reputedly on 5/- which his family never believed. He came to Stockton from Birstall near Leeds to become the first machine shop foreman with Pickerings Lifts, who incidentally are still operating.

The early days had their humour. 'F.T.' started with a small drilling machine and a little hand drill in what was called in the old days 'the washhouse' which had a wooden hatch opening out on to the back street. The old lady next door took umbrage and for a week or two she would open this door and put a shovel full of cinders onto the machines. 'F.T.', being a very strong character, impressed her with the seriousness of it and it was discontinued.

'F.T.' built a very small shop in brick at the bottom of the back street adjoining Lustrum Beck and this building remained until the company vacated it in 1948. Fred Harker, grandson of old 'F.T.', comments "On reflection, the building and all the machines should really have been presented to the Beamish Museum in Durham."

'F.T.' was a very good engineer and at times brilliant. He designed his own steam engines and boats and built both. He was very fortunate in having three sons who entered the business and served apprenticeships each one of whom was a craftsman in his own right and spent his whole working life in the family business.

In the early stages they built small boats and small marine engines (steam) then as they bought new machines, i.e. belt driven, they began to make larger engines, the largest one they ever made weighing 14 tons. How they managed to do this is unclear as they had no overhead crane and no lifting capacity beyond block and tackle. On this

Above: Francis Todd Harker, 'Old F.T.' the founder of the company, with his wife, Jane pictured at the turn of the century. Known as a strong-willed man, 'F.T.' had many an argument with his three sons during his years as director of the company.
Below: The 'Gondolier' was built and engined by 'F.T.' for his pleasure, before WW1. This photo was taken at the mouth of the River Tees.

occasion they drilled the cylinders and the cylinder covers with a brace and bit up in the pattern loft.

In those days wages were so low, maybe no more than £1 per week, that it was not a critical cost. 'F.T' never employed more than seven or eight men. He was a very strong, dominating, character and the shop being so small everyone worked at full pressure. The best employee of all by far, and equal to any of the three brothers, was Tom Coggins who remained with the firm for 50 years. He came to the new premises in 1948 when they were complete and worked for a year or two before retiring.

'F.T.'s' three sons (Hubert, Harry and Jack) worked for a considerable time for their father, who incidentally lived until he was 90, and when he was in his late 80s the three brothers

Above and left: Two early examples of the company's engines. The above picture is of a 14 ton engine built in the 1920s. The picture on the left is from slightly earlier and shows two members of the Harker family, Frank and Winnie, Fred's cousins. Winnie is now 91 and lives in Montreal, Canada.

tried to persuade him to hand the business over to them. The argument went on for some considerable time but 'F.T.' would not relent. Finally they went on strike which lasted many months. In the end 'F.T.' conceded, handed the business over to them, plus the debts that had been incurred during this period. It took them many years of hard work to pay these off.

Fred Harker (The father of the current managing director, Malcolm and son of Hubert) recalls "The old belt driven machines and the gas lamps around the shop with small gas pipes and flexible arms and gas mantels. If there was a lot of vibration they would break and that would incur wrath from father. It was quite an incredible atmosphere but the work they turned out was superb."

Sadly, Harry Harker was the first to die, in his late 50s, Jack Harker died when he was 74 and Hubert, Fred's father, lived until 95 and was able to see the firm prosper and be in a position to move out into a much larger building and install new modern machines. This was in 1948 and ever since the company has progressed year by year, nothing spectacular but solid and steady.

Fred remembers "In 1929/1930, probably at the depth of the recession, the gross turnover of Harkers was 30/-. The only reason Harkers survived was because

Jack Harker was a thrifty person and was determined that the business should not die. Each day throughout the whole year he would go down to see if there was any mail or if there was an order, which there never was. Finally the following year Stockton Technical College (maybe they knew of the company's predicament) gave Harkers an order to build a small steam engine for their heat engine laboratory in Nelson Terrace. This was the turning point."

As the 1939-46 war approached the company became busier and during the war they built steam engines for the Admiralty, also bomb carriers, and a lot of other work connected with the war effort.

During the war Hubert and his son, Fred, corresponded regularly and after a year or two Hubert began to suggest that Fred should come home from India and join the family business. Incidentally, many years before, Fred's mother, who knew she would not live very long, made Hubert promise that under no circumstances whatever would Fred enter the family business. "Throughout her married life she had seen

Above: Jack Harker, one of the three brothers who took over from their father, 'F.T.' can be seen on the right of this picture. The engine was built for Thomas Cook and was installed on a pleasure steamer on the Nile!

the tears and sweat, and apparently did not wish me to experience the same hardships. Hence I went to India in 1938 for eight years. From being a young boy of six I was brain-washed into Harkers Engineering business and deep down I always yearned to see it rise from the ashes. Happily my father lived long enough to see this happen, this was very rewarding " recalls Fred. Fred's first experience on his return was the shock of seeing all the old belt driven machines and everything exactly the same as the day he left England eight years previously.

despatched to the Bridge Road Depot for transport all over the world, 'F.T.' would insist on waiting for a nice day. The engines were superb to look at and he insisted on a flat top wagon pulled by two, sometimes four, shire horses. It was a magnificent sight. 'F.T.' would walk 50 yards behind the carriage to hear people saying what a magnificent engine it was.

During one of these times a Brougham with two Palomino horses pulled alongside and Sir Leonard Ropner, head of Ropner ship building family,

However, Fred had burnt his boats and realised that the only thing to do was to put his head down and work hard. The great longing he had to return to India still lingers to this day. It was a wonderful life for a young bachelor.

dismounted and walked alongside 'F.T.' expressing his admiration. He then turned to the younger man and said that it was a beautiful engine and asked if he could put money into the business and make it grow. 'F.T.' thanked Sir Leonard but said there was only room for "one old bugger" in his business. Sir Leonard was highly amused. He mounted the Brougham and carried on his way to his shipyard in Stockton, not many yards from where the company now has its machine shops.

Throughout the whole of the life span of building marine engines (steam) Harkers had a tremendously high reputation throughout the British Isles, in fact they were referred to as the Rolls Royce of steam engines. Unfortunately, Francis Todd Harker did not take full advantage of this. Instead of the business growing, as every other engineering business did between 80 and 100 years ago, he more or less stood still. His main and only interest was in building engines, not making the business expand.

> "ON FRED'S RETURN FROM INDIA HE WAS SHOCKED TO FIND NOTHING HAD CHANGED IN HIS EIGHT YEARS AWAY."

Following this period of good fortune it became a little more difficult to obtain orders for steam engines to keep a continuity of work. Therefore what happened would be nine months of feverish activity, the three brothers working five nights a week until 9 o'clock, and the other craftsmen working three nights a week. In those early days Saturday up till 5 o' clock was the norm.

During one spell they built engines for the Aire and Calder Navigation Company in Leeds and this association lasted for 10 years. Fred remembers "When they were nearing completion of an engine Grandfather would write to them and ask for another order as the engine was almost complete, and lo and behold in a weeks time an order would pop through the letterbox. Like all good things this finally came to an end." Whenever an engine was complete and was to be

Towards the end of the 1920s orders were very intermittent and life was by no means easy as many years there would be a period of three or four months when there was no work available. These days it is

Above: An engine from the very early days being guarded by a local young man in the lane behind the works.

very difficult to appreciate the hardships of those times.

On one occasion when there had been no work for approximately six months they received an order from agents in Liverpool called Jones Burton, which meant working flat out because most of these orders had a premium attached to the price, it operated both ways. If you were late you lost it and if early you benefited. In all cases they benefited. In the first week of this particular order the three brothers worked five nights a week and one worker, Tom Coggins worked alongside them and when Hubert gave him his wage packet he refused it. Fred recounts "Father was baffled and passed it back. He told Tom it was his wages, including overtime. He replied that he knew that the three brothers had worked the same hours without taking any extra money out. Father pointed out that the Union rules said that he had to be paid. However, Tom had his way and received for the rest of that period of time the same wages as father and Uncle Jack. They were much lower than those to which he was due. In Tom's old age the company was able to show their appreciation for his tremendous loyalty and long service."

On the same lines another interesting and touching occasion was when Harry Harker was terminally ill with cancer and as he always turned the crankshafts he insisted that he finished the job before he retired to his bed for the last time. Hubert and Jack pleaded

with him to go home but he would not heed them so they propped him up in a Windsor chair with cushions and he lived long enough to finish the job. This day and age it seems almost unbelievable but it does describe the loyalty that was very prevalent.

Hubert was the only one of the three brothers who would stand up to 'F.T.', the founder. The running battle continued for many years and was never really resolved. In the latter stages Harry said to him "I wish you and father would not row so much, although I know you are fully entitled to do so, but he will never give in and he won't live for ever." Father in later years used to add "The old bugger nearly did!" recalls Fred. Harry Harker was a first class designer, craftsman and draftsman. Jack was a superb craftsman who could turn his hand to anything. Hubert was the driving force. In fact all the men who worked for him would say the slave driver. Strange to relate they all had the highest regard for him because he never bore anyone a grudge. Incidentally, to work in the old machine shop off Norton Road was an experience no one would ever forget, it had an atmosphere entirely of its own.

The company moved out of Danby road in 1948 into a new building in Church Road thanks to a loan of £6,000 from Stockton Corporation and the following year the company bought its first new machine in 50 years, a Ward 7 Turret Lathe. At 9.25pm on the day of delivery Ruth, Fred's wife rang to say "It is time you

> ## "IN 1949 THE COMPANY BOUGHT ITS FIRST NEW MACHINE FOR OVER 50 YEARS. IT WAS A TIME OF CELEBRATION."

stopped stroking that machine. Come home!". It was the forerunner of many, many more as the business began to grow. Each year or two it expanded, not dramatically but sensibly. No.2 shop was built and within two years was full of the best machines we could buy. At one stage every machine in this shop was less than five years old.

On one occasion Fred remembers saying to Ken Monkhouse, the machine shop Manager "Isn't life bloody dull" in other words he had no justification for buying a machine. "The night I made this remark Ken and I began to throw ideas about until 9.30pm. The following night we continued our discussion and lo and behold we decided to build No. 3 shop and the new offices. When everything was buzzing I had to supervise all the building and do everything in the office and the works with help from a small staff. At the height of all this activity, Ken turned to me and said 'Is life still bloody dull?'"

The reason the company is still in business is the fact it has ploughed all the profits back into the business and kept right up to date.

Malcolm Harker, fourth generation of the family, now runs the company and has done so for 20 years with a break for 6/7 years when he was in America but he is back and has Harkers' blood in his body. He found it too strong to resist. Fred still goes to the office every day, which he says is what "keeps me youngish!"

All the machines now are fully computerised. and the company employ 150 people, 50 years ago it was 7 or 8 but however large it grows it will always remain a family business 119 years old. With a strength of character so obvious in all the Harker men, this policy is set to come true. Long may it remain.

Recent Highlights
- *In 1987 the company was honoured with a visit from Prince Charles and Margaret Thatcher.*
- *In 1991 it won The Queens Award for Export Achievement.*
- *Malcolm also received the MBE in 1991.*
- *In 1995 Fred Harker received an honorary Master of Science Degree from the University of Teeside which was presented to him by Sir Leon Brittan the Chancellor.*

We now work for one of the largest businesses in America - 'G.E.' and other contracts include Germany, Poland, France (Arianne rocket), plus various branches of Rolls Royce. Needless to say we are highly thought of.

Fred comments "I had a truly wonderful wife, Ruth (nee Wilkinson) she supported me in every way possible. She never complained even when I arrived home at 9.50pm five nights per week for nearly 30 years. On rare occasions it was 10pm, she would say 'No lodgers tonight!'"

One of the Golden Gems the three brothers left Fred when he joined in 1946 was a superb reputation for quality and honest dealing. A wonderful start for a young man of 36 to build on and something that has led the company through hardships and will continue to lead it into the new millennium.

Below: Fred Harker, his daughter Jillian and son Malcolm who now runs the company.
Facing page: Three generations of the Harker family from left to right: Ruth, Fred's wife with baby Katia, Malcolm, Fred, Jillian and director Alan Kitching. Jillian's twin sons, Peter and Richard, are ready to throw the switch to 'launch' the Harker Engine with a bottle of champagne on the occasion of the firm's centenary.

The birth of British Visqueen

The Yarm Road, Stockton business, British Visqueen is a world leader among makers of polythene films. However it has made a name for itself in many other markets. A wide range of its films are used in the building trade, for example damp-proof membranes to protect structures and heavy-duty fertiliser sacks and silage film in the agricultural industry.

Its story began in the early 1950s with a chance meeting, on a voyage on the Queen Mary, between the head of the Visking Corporation of America and the then chairman of ICI's Plastics Division, Sir Peter

Allen. Sir Peter recognised the potential of the 'bubble-blowing' process to manufacture a thin and uniform film from polythene granules. The merger that resulted between ICI polymers and American 'know-how' led to the mass-production of polythene film to make sacks, bags and other products which have since become part of everyday life.

The Stockton factory is built on a 25 acre site, well served by the railway and previously rented to an American owned company that dealt in earth-moving machinery and later by Metro-Vick-Peacock-Baver who built Diesel electric locomotives. In 1961, recession drove this latter firm to concentrate on their Manchester factory. Its Stockton factory lay idle for a year before being bought by British Visqueen Ltd.

The UK company too had had a varied history, beginning near Blackpool. The first major factory was established at Stevenage where films for packaging, mainly of food products were developed. In the sixties new investment extended use of the film for agricultural and horticultural purposes. When the agricultural division developed Nitram it needed the protection of a polythene sack to keep the fertiliser dry and free-flowing. This was the purpose of the new plant in Stockton-on-Tees

quality covers for the large tunnels in which mushrooms are grown and films to cover the ground around crops, and clinical waste sacks!

The plant, now part of British Polythene Industries, has been re-structured into four companies, Films, Sacks, Agri and Refuse. The management believes that the new arrangement gives a better focus on the four separate areas and making the four businesses more cost effective. Agri, Films and Sacks have already gained Investor in People status and Refuse will follow.

which opened in 1962 to make a range of 'Polisax' for the fertiliser industry.

The company is environmentally responsible. It has carried out a survey on the types of plants in the 20-acre grounds around the plant to enable them better to plan ways of further improving conditions for wild life in the area.

Since 1962 many changes have occurred with new products being introduced and old ones being phased out. For a number of years, woven polypropylene sacks were manufactured on the site. In 1971 the manufacture of refuse sacks became an integral part of the site serving many local Councils with black polythene refuse sacks. There are now many strings to Visqueen's bow. It makes the bags in which Freemans' catalogue goods are delivered to your door; it makes high

Above: British Visqueen's factory at Stockton.
Top left: Visqueen 1200. Polyethylene sheeting being used as an oversite membrane.
Centre left: The factory entrance.
Left: The factory from the air showing its position in relation to Stockton.
Facing page, top: Strings being tied on woven polypropylene sacks.
Facing page, centre: One of the largest single-site sack manufacturing plants in Europe.
Facing page, bottom: A lorry loaded with the first consignment of sacks for Billingham.

The benefits of bulk buying

The John Russell in the title of the firm John Russell & Son (Grocers) Ltd. never actually worked in the business but he provided the capital for his son Steven to set up the original shop. It was situated in Oxford Street, Stockton, was first opened in 1895 and remained the family's business premises for 67 years. It was a two-storey building with space for spare stock on the upper floor. Pulleys lifted it and there was a chute for getting goods back down to the shop again when they were required.

Work was hard and long but Russells offered a service that persuaded the people from the surrounding houses to become regular customers and the business did well. Deliveries were made with a pony and trap.

The firm turned to wholesaling in a small way in 1914 and it gradually grew to the point where they were able to begin to operate the buying group RAFT in 1959. The business was served in turn by Frank Bell, and his son Jim, Margaret Morrison and her son Donald, Ian Bell is the present M.D.

RAFT is a 'buying in bulk' facility that helped the independent grocer to compete with the multiple dealers. The initials stand for Russell Association of Free Traders and RAFT shops are to be found throughout Darlington, Teesside, Cleveland County and Northallerton. Helped by a cash-and-carry buying group, now called Sterling Supergroup, Russells became well known for 'Sterling' labelled products. A weekly

Above: Going to an exhibition, Mr Frank Bell is fifth from the right.
Left: Mrs Margaret Morrison makes a presentation to Hilda Lough whilst other employees of John Russell look on.

round of special offers together with window bills and other posters helped shopkeepers compete against the ever growing power of the supermarket. This was supplemented by a consultancy service on any aspect of the devel-

opment of a member's shop, for example the best self-service layouts or fittings. If required, Russells actually carried out the work. A fleet of vans made weekly deliveries in whichever way best suited each individual customer. There was also a catering division. The move to Portrack Lane was made in 1962 and the area of coverage was increased when R Best & Sons, the Middlesbrough

wholesale grocers joined Russells in 1965.

The activities of RAFT are still flour- ishing today but Russell's realise that the job of a whole- saler is continually changing. Twenty

years ago the independent grocer had over 50% of the grocery market. It has now declined to less than 8%. The company intends to continue its diversification into new areas of the market. At present their business is growing in the areas of goods for the catering trade and in frozen foods. The hand cart and the trap gave way many years ago to push bikes and then motorised vehicles. Nowadays, of course, the movements of vans, fork lift trucks and lorries are dictated by computer and the company is served by every relevant modern device.

Above: *The Portrack Lane premises of John Russell & Son.*
Top: *Mr Jim Bell is on the left on Russells stand at the Middlesbrough Licensed Victuallers Association in April 1967.*
Below: *On this picture of The Bowwater-Scott Corporation taken in June 1962, Mr Jim Bell, father of Russell's present managing director, is to be seen fourth from the left on the back row.*

The family business that is recycling today to preserve the future

The well known company of L Bainbridge & Sons was established in 1941 by Leslie and Selina (Lena) Bainbridge. Leslie was one of seven children and had served his time as a butcher, working in his father's shop until, after being left an orphan at the age of fourteen, the family decided to sell the shop, as it wasn't providing a living. He spent the next few years exploring all kinds of avenues to make ends meet and he decided it was time to think about his own dreams and ambitions. Together with his wife, he found premises in Portrack Lane, known as The Villas and began a business dismantling vehicles for spare parts and selling the residue for scrap. World War II was an opportune time for such a business, as new vehicle parts were almost impossible to get hold of.

Despite this, the family still struggled to keep their heads above water and Leslie and Lena grew potatoes and other arable crops on their farm to support the war effort in growing food on their land. Cyril, their eldest son aquired a potato licence to sell their crops, as well as keeping livestock. As coal was on ration during the war, Cyril used to sell logs and delivered orders for grocery shops. After school, his father would have his three ponies saddled up and he would take them around the streets of Stockton, charging local children a penny a ride, going further afield at weekends to the nearby seasides of Saltburn and Seaton Carew giving donkey and horse rides on the sands. All the family helped and worked extremely hard as a team to make a shilling during those bleak times.

As the effects of the war receded, the family could spend more time concentrating on the business. The children, Cyril and Leslie Junior became more involved in the day-to-day running of it.

Leslie, Lena and Leslie Junior took care of the car sales whilst Cyril expanded on the Auto Spares section, which led to the aquisition of CL Prosser & Co. Ltd in 1953. In the early

Top: *Miss Wallace, T. R. Bainbridge's auntie, Mr Timothy Ruecroft Bainbridge and their apprentice outside the shop in 1897.* **Above left:** *Family members at the opening of Norton motors in 1967, from left to right: Mrs Lena Bainbridge, Mr J. W. Mason, Cyril Bainbridge, Mr and Mrs R. Wilson.* **Above right:** *At the same event left to right, Mr Gatenby, Tim Bainbridge, Mr Doug Jones, Leslie Bainbridge Sr, Bruce Forsyth and Cyril Bainbridge.* **Left:** *A family outing in 1962 with a young Robert holding Grandma Lena's hand and Dorothy Bainbridge with the white handbag.*

export world wide. Customers range from house-holders to major national companies and the company has recently expanded again into demolition and industrial dismantling and running a comprehensive waste and skip hire service.

Recycling is the way of the world today and with this thought in mind, it is with recycling that the future will be preserved, CL Prosser now provide recyclable materials which are then processed into useable raw materials.

years of CL Prosser there was hardly any machinery used, most activities were carried out manually, as time progressed and the business grew materials were processed by mechanical alligator shears and transported to steel works by railway trucks.

L. Bainbridge and Sons Ltd. remained at Portrack Lane until 1976, whilst building a further garage and car sale showroom in 1967 known as Norton Motors, on Norton Road, Stockton. Both the garages were sold in the late 1970's and CL Prosser & Co. Ltd was

expanded which lead to the purchase of a depot at South Bank, Middlesbrough, allowing the company to provide a service in the metals recycling industry throughout the North East of England.

Nowadays, CL Prosser supplies ferrous and non-ferrous metals to steelworks and foundries throughout the United Kingdom and in recent years the company has obtained outlets for material for

Three generations of the Bainbridge family have now been at the helm of the company and the youngest members think back with pride on their parents and grandparents efforts, sharing in this determination to succeed and appreciate the hard work of their family as they did the groundwork which helped build the company into what it is today. Today the tradition continues and the company contributes strongly in the metals recycling industry, whilst giving employment to 40 people, it endeavours to maintain steady expansion and grows on the strength of its reputation.

Top: Another picture from the opening of Norton Motors in 1967 with, back row: Theresa Bainbridge, Ernie Moonie, Maureen Bainbridge, Cyril Bainbridge, Harry Dowling, Leslie Bainbridge Sr, John W Mason, Leslie Bainbridge Jr and two colleagues. Front row: Tim Bainbridge, Robert Lawson, Mary Dowling and Alan Cash. **Above left:** *Villa Car Sales in the late 1960s.* **Above:** *A newspaper advert for L Bainbridge & Sons from 1964 showing prices for popular cars of the day.* **Left:** *The yard of CL Prosser & Co at South Bank, Middlesbrough in 1969.* **Below:** *The Directors of CL Prosser today from left to right: Ronnie Bainbridge, Lena Bainbridge Jr, Cyril Bainbridge and Robert Bainbridge.*

From a Belgian Black to a Silver Ghost

It was in 1870 that joiner and cabinet maker Joseph Relph set himself up in business as a funeral director. His premises were in Boundary Road, Middlesbrough and in the early days all his coffins were made of solid timber. Nowadays timber is only used for very expensive coffins whilst cheaper ones are made of veneered chipboard.

There have been changes too in the way the coffins are transported. In the 1870s Joseph Relph would go to the bakers' shops in Cannon Street to hire horses for funerals. A Belgian Black horse was a particular favourite.

During the journey a whip had to be kept handy to keep the horses moving. Otherwise they would automatically stop at the bakers' premises expecting their wagons to be loaded with loaves and cakes. A man was employed to 'page' or walk in front of the horse. He had a permanent sheen on the back of his black coat from stopping and having the horse walk into his back.

The firm has been entrusted with the funeral arrangements for a number of prestigious people, for example Sir Joseph William Isherwood and, in April 1929, Dr Lacey the Bishop of Middlesbrough, and they have buried no less than four Roman Catholic bishops.

For most of this century, of course, coffins and mourners have been driven in dignified black cars. These have included Rolls Royces and a Silver Ghost.

The firm is a member of the National Association of Funeral Directors and the British Institute of embalmers. Its specialities include embalming and repatriation work.

Above: The Belgian Black horse harnessed to a splendid and dignified carriage. The officials look suitably solemn but the small girl visible under the horse's belly is unimpressed, giving all her attention to her doll's pram.
Above left: An early advertisement mentioning the head office in Borough Road West and branch office in Robson Street, Haverton Hill It offers the firm's cars for all occasions as well as funeral services with distance no object.
Left: An impressive line-up of Rolls .

A true taste of tradition

Richard Lazenby founded the Company, with the help of his wife Rosemary, in 1982, following a highly successful career in catering. He had previously established his own range of mustards and pickles and after experimenting with pates and cooked meats, recognised that there was a highly neglected product niche, that of quality traditional sausages.

1996. The Company has succeeded throughout 1997 to utilise its traditional and flexible manufacturing skills, product innovation capabilities and keen customer negotiating methods to consistently outmanoeuvre the competition and remain Market leaders in their sector.

After creating a reputation for the products with multiple retailers, the business grew to a point where the original premises in Stokesley (comprising 7,000 sq ft) provided insufficient capacity to satisfy national demand.

In 1993 the Company relocated to the present unit at Thornaby, which provided 27,000 sq ft and within eighteen months it was necessary to increase the working area by a further 3,500 sq feet.

Since year ending 31 January 1990, the Company has increased its annual turnover from £1.0m to £8.57 m for year ending 31 January 1996. Turnover for year ending 31 January 1997 increased slightly to £8.9m representing a solid year's trading.

1996 was an extremely important year for the Company as, with any growing business it was necessary to face new challenges; not only within the Market from increased competition, but internally, in terms of structuring the business in order to allow it to compete with multi-national operations.

Valda Morris was initially appointed as Operations Director in January 1996, with a brief to address this one major issue. She has since carried out an extensive development exercise on the business and has succeeded in greatly improving efficiencies, market position and management effectiveness. Valda was promoted to Managing Director in December

The key to success for Mr Lazenby's is Quality, in terms of the sourcing of raw materials, production

methods, presentation and people. The Company consistently refuses to enter into business where customers require a 'low quality' product to suit a 'low price' market and in doing this, maintains its leading position as the best quality sausage producer in Great Britain. The BBC Good Food Magazine, recently reiterated this by stating that Mr Lazenby's sausage is 'The British Banger at its best'. The future for Mr Lazenby's is one of planned further improvement in Market positioning, continued innovation in product and packaging development, and solid financial growth.

Top: The Stokesley staff celebrating hygiene certification in 1986.
Above left: A 1983 photograph of Richard with one of the early range of pickles.
Above: One of the new fleet of distinctive delivery lorries.
Left: Richard Lazenby with his famous sausages in the 1990s.

A proud tradition of quality education

Red House School is an independent, co-educational junior, preparatory and senior day school educating children from four to sixteen years.

The school was founded in 1929 at Ragworth Hall, Norton, by Mrs Phillips of Norton and Mrs Kenny of Marton, following a series of meetings between eight local women concerned about the lack of good kindergarten and preparatory education in the area. It opened with a total of 28 pupils, many of whose parents formed the governing body. The first headmaster was Mr Bertram Surtees Raine who stayed with Red House until 1964. The school flourished under his guidance and that of his wife and the number of pupils grew steadily.

In 1933 the school became a limited company with charitable status- all surplus income being devoted to the improvement of the school and its

equipment. In 1938, 130 pupils moved to Red House which was purchased for £2,500. On the outbreak of war in 1939 the pupils were evacuated to Barnard Castle School and then in 1940 to Whorlton Hall. The kindergarten remained at Red House

A charming 1930s photograph of the whole school with Mr Raine in the centre in the dark suit.

and, after the war, the whole school was re-united and continued to go from strength to strength thanks to the devoted work of Mr and Mrs Raine.

Steady growth continued with the building of a new assembly hall and a new wing containing a science laboratory, classrooms and changing rooms. It was opened by and named after Bertram Surtees Raine in 1969

The old vicarage was purchased at the beginning of the 1980s to house the junior school and a senior school opened in 1983 to accommodate 13 to 16 year olds. In recent years an extensive building programme has seen the addition of a sports hall, changing rooms and showers, new classrooms, the library, four science laboratories - all able to accommodate the 420 pupils.

Education at Red House takes place in a caring environment where outstanding academic achievements are matched on the playing fields, in music, art and creative writing, with great emphasis placed on the social values nurtured by Mr and Mrs Raine; tolerance and respect for each other.

Facing page, top left: Mr B Surtees Raine . Mr Raine was headmaster of the school between 1929 and 1964. Facing page, top right: The pocket motif from the 1935-36 term. Above: Little description is necessary for this delightful 1930s picture of the school cricket eleven. Right: Mr England, the current Headmaster.

Committed to continuous improvement

In 1973 the County Borough of Teesside closed the grammar schools of Stockton-on-Tees and established 11-16 comprehensives. The Secretary of State for Education at the time, Mrs Margaret Thatcher, was then invited to open the first purpose-built sixth form college in the north of England in Stockton.

In the time since then the town has had reason to be proud of its college's achievements. It has admirably fulfilled its primary function of being a bridge between O-levels, now G.C.S.E.s, and university entrance for pupils who would have stayed on in their pre

1973 schools, enabling many hundreds of young people to study for a degree. However, from the beginning the college has offered far more. To school leavers who had rejected the university

option it represented the opportunity to study for qualifications to obtain interesting and challenging work. To those who had begun to regret wasting their schooldays it represented a

deal with all matters concerning its staff, the maintenance of its buildings and its facilities.

Its independent status gives the college complete control of its own curriculum. This already covered the traditional range of subjects. Since incorporation it has the freedom to respond to the wishes and interests of the wider Stockton community. A-levels are still the largest single area of the college's work with all the traditional subjects still offered and popular. However, new and increasingly favoured choices include Business Studies, Computing, Law, Psychology and Sociology.

second chance to obtain G.C.S.E.s and other qualifications.

For twenty years the college worked under local government control. After that, the Further and Higher Education Act of 1992 established Stockton Sixth Form College as an educational corporation, funded by the Further Education Funding Council in Coventry. Members of the local business community, the University College in Stockton, a representative from the Teesside Training and Enterprise Council, together with staff and parents make up the college corporation.

"ITS INDEPENDENT STATUS GIVES THE COLLEGE COMPLETE CONTROL OF ITS OWN CURRICULUM"

These are the people who now decide on the mission aims and objectives of the college. They also manage its financial affairs,

Facing page top: The college library pictured in 1974.
Facing page bottom: The college as it appeared on the front of the 1974 prospectus.
Above: The lounge as it was when the college first opened.
Right: Modern technology assists in fitness measurement on the Sports Science course.

Vocational courses are now offered and these provide specialised studies in order to prepare a student to enter a particular career. Examples of these are the BTEC Diplomas in Sports and Science and GNVQs in Health and Social Care, Business, Information Technology and Leisure and Tourism.

Students are mainly in the 16-19 age range. However, the Further and Higher Education Act also gave the college an opportunity to provide adults with the chance to gain new skills and qualifications through part-time

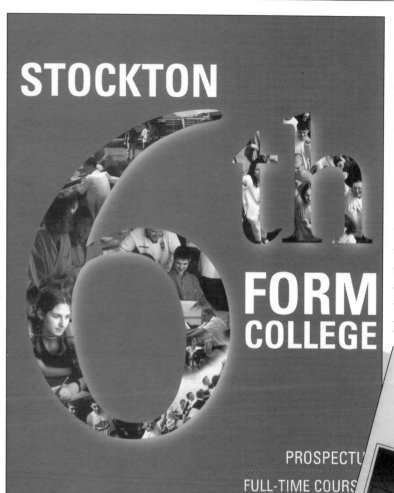

STOCKTON
6th
FORM
COLLEGE

PROSPECTU

FULL-TIME COURS

1998/

The
New Stocktonian

1989 - 1990

ensure the best possible academic success, the college has set itself wider aims. Work placements during some study programmes are only one kind of link between the college and local industry. Modern Language students are offered work shadowing in Strasbourg. There is a well-established student exchange system with the Lycée Auguste Renoir in Stockton's twin French town, Asnieres.

The college has a special arrangement with a local organisation, the Dovecot Arts Centre. This allows students to play, compose or record contemporary music under the guidance and expert tuition of professional musicians.

Many students find time to round off their learning experiences by undertaking regular voluntary work in primary schools, residential homes and day care centres in the borough. There is a good range of sporting facilities on college premises, including a large sports

further education. An average 500 adult students each year take up courses of study leading to A-levels, GCSEs and also both introductory and more advanced courses in Information Technology and Computing. Classes are held both during the day and in the evenings.

In 1973 the college began with a total of 500 16-19 year olds, now, in 1997 the total is 1,200 young people and adults. The college is proud not only of the high quality of its teaching but also of the professional guidance and specialist career support that its students are offered.

The excellent report given to Stockton Sixth Form College in 1996 by the Further Education Funding Council was not unexpected by people who knew the college well. Inspectors were particularly impressed with the standard of education provided in all areas of the curriculum, with staff professionalism and commitment to improvement. This view of the college was supported by its Investment in People Award in 1997.

Having set in place everything necessary to

hall. The students also have access to other specialist sports facilities. Many students compete at county level in soccer, hockey and rugby. College teams are well respected, even feared, in regional events and competitions. A small number

Above: College publications include the latest college prospectus on the left which reflects the professional and independent status of Stockton Sixth Form college. The New Stocktonian, pictured right is the house magazine for former students, an annual reminder of past and current achievements and activities.
Facing page top: Activities featured in the current prospectus which illustrate the wide range of studies and recreational facilities available to students.
Facing page bottom: Gillian Shepherd MP, meets students from the college at the House of Commons in 1995.

local authority, at a number of community centres throughout the borough.

The college's pride in its past is well balanced by its plans for the future. It has an ambitious programme of investment in Information Technology to help Stockton prepare itself for the demands of the 21st century. As its Silver Jubilee approaches in 1998 its objectives are all the ones it began with in 1973, to provide and extend opportunities for over-sixteens in an environment in which every individual counts.

of students have represented their country in international sporting competitions.

Its independence has not separated the college from other educational institutions in the town. Obviously it has close contact with its partner schools, encouraging young people to extend their education. The college co-operates closely with Stockton's adult Education Service offering a wide range of opportunities to mature students. In the scheme known as 'New Start Course for Women' the college works in partnership with the

Education built on strong traditions

In Tudor times Stockton was a small village in the parish of Norton. Norton had a Grammar School catering for 50 boys and with a headmaster in Holy Orders.

By 1712 Stockton had grown sufficiently to become a parish in its own right and the Stockton Charity, or Blue Coat School was established there in 1721. A Church of England foundation, it educated 20 boys by voluntary subscription, religious instruction and the inculcation of civilised behaviour taking precedence over academic subjects.

The school prospered modestly and a legacy, received in 1819 provided a new and better building. The town continued to grow and other church schools began to spring up. It occurred to enlightened benefactors that Stockton should have a grammar school.

In 1882 several gentlemen joined themselves to form a limited company and raised enough money to open a mixed-sex High School. Finance was tight and staff and pupils suffered some hardships but Mr Vie, the headmaster was able and dedicated.

In 1894 the Blue Coat elementary School closed. Its endowment was now to provide secondary education for 38 elementary school boys. These and the pupils of the High School formed the new Stockton Grammar School which took over the Blue Coat premises. More pupils came from Norton when the Tudor Grammar School closed. Stockton Grammar School opened in 1895. Its girls were later transferred to the Queen Victoria High School in Yarm Road.

Following the 1902 Education Act the County Secondary School was opened. It was twice the size of the Grammar School, modern and purpose-built. It was a daunting challenge to the Grammar School. Mr Vie, its head was still dedicated but no longer in his youth and full vigour.

It was under his successor, Mr R I Glasspool that the now traditional system of houses, prefects and school societies was introduced. Masters were lost to war

Top: Unveiling the War Memorial, 8th May 1956.
Centre: The Headteacher of the New School (Stockton Grammar School) in Fairfield Road, Mr. F.W. Cain B.A. 1963
Right: The opening and dedication of the New School by the Archbishop of York, Dr. Donald Coggan on the 11th October 1963.

was then opened by the Archbishop of York, Dr Coggan, on a greenfield site in Fairfield in 1963.

In the sixties, when the 11+ examination fell into disfavour, Stockton opted for 11-16 comprehensive schools with a 6th form college. The Grammar school became one of the former and was renamed the **Ian Ramsey School** after a distinguished Bishop of Durham who died in office.

service in 1914. The school employed lady teachers and the part time services of neighbouring clergy. Between the wars the school's academic reputation grew but its facilities left much to be desired and its mere one-form entry meant no 'option' subjects were possible until the 6th form.
Some improvements to the buildings and equipment were possible in 1936 when ICI was developing at Billingham and pupils were keen to study science. The school managed to survive the stresses and deprivations of the second war but after it came Rab Butler's Education Act. As Durham County planned to implement it, it could see no place for a tiny grammar school.

Headmaster Thomas Ridley studied the text of the Act and claimed Aided status for his school as an institution of the C of E. This meant it received a 50% government grant towards rebuilding costs. Together with generous help from some successful Old Boys, there was enough money to rebuild the school which

Established in 1972 by amalgamation with Fairfield Secondary School, it presently caters for 1223 11-16 year olds who proceed, if they wish, to Stockton 6th Form College. They are taught by 70 staff in buildings which are modern, well equipped and maintained by the Church of England. The governing body, which includes several clergymen, is very supportive.

The Ian Ramsey C. of E. School today is noted for its sound academic achievement, high standards in sport and opportunities offered in music and extra curricular activities. The school tries hard to live up to the traditions of the past.

Top: Ian Ramsey Church of England School Chapel, opened in 1963.
Centre: 1982 National School Hockey Champions.
Above: The 1997 School Rugby Team.
Left: The school entrance .

Deep roots and new growth - the story of Grangefield School

These 'Deep Roots' in fact began in January 1896, when the Stockton School Board opened its Higher Grade School in Nelson Terrace, Stockton. The Higher Grade School provided a good basic education for all its pupils despite the problems that the Headteacher, Mr J. J. Prest describes in the School Log Book for 1896 where he wrote, "The intelligence of more than one half of the girls is below the average for ordinary elementary scholars."

The present Grangefield School has built on this foundation and provides a 'broad, balanced and relevant curriculum' for all its pupils. This was recognised when the school was awarded the Schools Curriculum Award in 1987. The award recognised 'the school at the heart of the community' and that provides another link with the past. School Log Books show how the school has always had a role in caring for its pupils' welfare. In January 1903, the Headteacher writes, "Eleven schools are receiving free breakfasts owing to lack of work in the town."

And in 1924 The Old Boys' Association organised a Christmas treat which was reminiscent of Charles Dickens' 'A Christmas Carol', "Swarms of lads all more or less ragged and unkempt but with light hearts and happy faces appeared from out of the wintry mist and vanished within the portals of the school. What a feast, ye gods, and what a clearance! The good things simply disappeared and a halt was called only when our little guests, with waistcoats open and buttons falling from their places, could eat no more."

The present school has two watch-words, one is 'Caring' and the other is 'Quality.' The quality of the education provided in the past century has often been tested.

Any modern school would be pleased to receive an Inspectors' Report like the one of March 1901, "The school is judiciously well organised and well-managed. The tone and discipline are highly praise-worthy and the instruction reflects great credit on the Headteacher and his staff."

Above: Mr Prest, first headmaster of the school in 1896.
Top left: The Stockton Higher Grade School opened in 1896.
Left: Miss Nelson, who took over the girls' side of the separated Higher Grade School in 1915.
Below: The female staff c1927.

In 1915, the school became two separate schools with Mr Prest as Headmaster of the Boys' School and Miss Nelson as Headmistress of the Girls' School.

The First World War saw pupils fighting for their country along with three members of staff. Ex-pupils of the Girls' School served as V.A.D.s in France and as Red Cross Nurses.

The War Memorial was unveiled in 1926 by Major General Sir Percival Wilkinson who said that, "The memorial would help those growing up to be worthy of the noble heritage that had come down to them." The school still holds a Remembrance Service every year to give modern pupils an opportunity to remember that 'noble heritage.'

The building in Nelson Terrace was becoming very dilapidated by the 1920s. A teacher described conditions, "There was no electricity until later and we had to stand on a desk seat, pull a long chain to turn on the gas. There was only cold water for washing for girls and staff. There was only a small, dusty macadamised playground and the staff room, was a low-ceilinged, glorified cupboard. .... Constant traffic noises and road-mending operations. In the earliest days we could hear the clanging of the ship-builders' hammers by the river."

However, plans for new schools on the Grange-field site had to be interrupted and left in abeyance as the Second World War approached. The skeleton walls of this so-called 'Ghost School' were to stand for many years before the buildings could be completed, in fact until 1951. The new Boys' School hall had a Second World War memorial, unveiled in 1952.

In the last forty years, the school has had many changes of name mostly due to educational reforms. In 1973, Comprehensive re-organisation led to the amalgamation of the two Grammar Schools into The Grange Comprehensive School.

In 1985, change continued when The Grange School was merged with another local Comprehensive, Sheraton School. This led to eighteen months of split-site working until a £2.5 million building programme was completed - a Sports Hall and Library were the outstanding features.

The Thomas Sheraton Library named after the famous furniture designer reminds us of the link between The

Above: The War Memorial, unveiled in 1926 by Major Sir Percival Wilkinson, in remembrance of those who lost their lives in the First World War.
Right: A charming 1920s picture of the school's cricket team.

Grange School and Sheraton School.
In 1989 Lord Stockton, grandson of Prime Minister Harold MacMillan, re-opened the newly refurbished school beginning a time of celebration including a large exhibition tracing the story of Grangefield School and universal education.

Among the more famous past pupils of the school are included Lord Mowbray-King speaker of the House of Commons, Pat Barker, a recent Booker Prize winner, world famous film director Ridley Scott and local radio and T.V. presenter, Paul Frost.

The Ofsted inspection of 1993 praised standards at the Grangefield School, but it would be hard to improve on the comments made by the School Inspectors in 1921, "Proud as have been the school records of the past, we are fully convinced from what we have seen this afternoon in the continued loyalty and intelligence of the

staff and the keen and happy interest of the pupils in their classwork, that there is an even greater future before our school." Let's hope that the future chapters in Grangefield's story continue this theme of growth and renewal in keeping with the school's motto 'Ex Glande Quercus - From Acorn to Oak.'

Above: A post Second World War picture of the boys' chemistry class.
Below: The Thomas Sheraton Library.